A Collins Intensive English Course

Compact

||| Intermediate

ENGLISH HOME TUITION SCHEME
21 DOBELL ROAD
LONDON SE9 1HE
TEL. 081 850 9459

Student's and Practice Book

Debra Powell *with*
Madeline McHugh

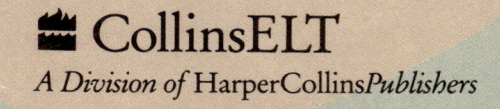

CollinsELT
A Division of HarperCollins*Publishers*

Contents and Map of the Book

SS = Student's Section PS = Practice Section
GR = Grammar Reference TS = Tapescripts

UNIT	TOPIC	STRUCTURES / LEXIS	FUNCTIONS
1 It's not what you say … SS page 1 PS page 41 GR page 61 TS page 66	non-verbal communication	S: infinitive of purpose L: participles as adjectives	expressing purpose; learning to understand body language
2 Rights of the child SS page 3 PS page 42 GR page 61 TS page 66	children's rights, ages of responsibility and charity work	S: gerund as subjects and objects L: opposites: prefixes un-, im-, il-, in-	giving permission; discussing rights
3 The senses SS page 5 PS page 43 GR page 61 TS page 67	the five senses	S: who/which in non-defining relative clauses L: phrasal verbs	giving additional information; describing the senses; giving your viewpoint
4 Read all about it! SS page 7 PS page 44 GR page 61 TS page 67	news stories and newspapers	S: present perfect v. past simple L: word groups: newspaper sections	discussing likes and dislikes; comparing newspaper styles
5 Young heroes SS page 9 PS page 45 GR page 61 TS page 68	modern-day heroes	S: adverbs of manner; by + -ing L: synonyms	talking about bravery; describing ways of doing things
6 A way of life SS page 11 PS page 46 GR page 62 TS page 68	lifestyles and traditions	S: not allowed to v. not supposed to; obligation/permission L: phrases	describing advantages/disadvantages; expressing permission; comparing tradition with modern lifestyles
7 Affairs of the heart SS page 13 PS page 47 GR page 62 TS page 69	relationships	S: first and second conditional L: synonyms and antonyms	giving advice; writing personal letters; describing people
8 The language of colour SS page 15 PS page 48 GR page 62 TS page 69	the effect of colour	S: pronouns in defining relative clauses L: word group: colours	discussing character; talking about colour associations
9 Service with a smile? SS page 17 PS page 49 GR page 62 TS page 70	aspects of service	S: the passive; by + agent L: multiple meaning words	making complaints
10 Men and women SS page 19 PS page 50 GR page 63 TS page 71	equality between the sexes	S: reason clauses: because and because of; causative make L: nouns to adjectives/suffixes -ness, -ity, -able, -ion, -ive	expressing opinions; agreeing and disagreeing

Unit 6 – W/b

UNIT	TOPIC	STRUCTURES / LEXIS	FUNCTIONS
11 Ceremonies & festivals SS page 21 PS page 51 GR page 63 TS page 71	ceremonies and festivals from around the world	S: causative *have*: *have X done, have had X done* L: word group: human / animal equivalents	talking about celebrations; discussing important events; giving a talk
12 The universe beyond SS page 23 PS page 52 GR page 63 TS page 72	space travel and the environment	S: future perfect L: vocabulary in context	describing future events; giving reasons; agreeing
13 Success and failure SS page 25 PS page 53 GR page 63 TS page 72	how to succeed and discussing success	S: third conditional L: lexical cohesion - equivalence	defining character; giving opinions; assessing importance
14 Future memory? SS page 27 PS page 54 GR page 63 TS page 72	dreams and their interpretation	S: direct and indirect speech L: reporting verbs: purpose and manner	agreeing and disagreeing; discussing personal experiences
15 Intentions and regrets SS page 29 PS page 55 GR page 64 TS page 73	childhood intentions	S: *was going to do*; *wish* + past perfect L: word group: posture	discussing unfulfilled intentions and regrets; giving reasons
16 The weather SS page 31 PS page 56 GR page 64 TS page 74	climatic effects on lifestyles and the environment	S: *if/unless* in first conditional clauses L: words for describing weather/seasons	giving opinions; giving warnings about the future; agreeing and disagreeing with a theory
17 You and your health SS page 33 PS page 57 GR page 64 TS page 74	alternative and conventional medicine	S: indirect questions/advice L: word groups: symptoms/illness, injury/treatment	expressing orders; filling in reports
18 Mysteries SS page 35 PS page 58 GR page 65 TS page 75	a murder story and literary categories	S: *could/may/might have done* L: three-word phrasal verbs with *get*	speculating about the past; solving mysteries; giving reasons
19 Places in time SS page 37 PS page 59 GR page 65 TS page 75	historic places and their landmarks	S: present perfect passive L: participles as adjectives of manner/degree	discussing preferences; talking about location; recognising features
20 Leaders SS page 39 PS page 60 GR page 65 TS page 76	what makes a leader?	S: *a/an/the*/zero article L: *a/an*	talking about personal qualities; using articles

UNIT 1

It's not what you say ...

1 Saying what you think

a Introduce yourself to the person sitting beside you. Note down what you said and what you did with your faces and bodies. Tell the class.

b In your country, what gestures do you use to mean:

Go away!   Come here!   That smells awful!   Be quiet!   Good luck!

In pairs, make a list of different ways of communicating without words.

2 Body language

a In pairs, answer the questions.

1 What facial expressions do you use when you are
   a) happy or pleased? b) sad or angry?
2 In your country, what gesture(s) do you use
   to mean a) no? b) yes?
3 What is the person in the drawing probably saying?

Non-verbal communication, or body language, refers to ways of communicating without words. Gesture, facial expression and posture are all forms of non-verbal communication. The meanings of some forms of body language are the same all over the world: when people are happy, they smile; when they are sad or angry, they frown or scowl. Nodding the head, or moving it up and down, is almost universally used to indicate 'yes'. Shaking the head from side to side to indicate 'no' is also a universal gesture and may be learned in infancy - when a baby has had enough milk, he turns his head from side to side to show he doesn't want any more. Shrugging the shoulders is another universal gesture used to show that a person does not know or understand what you are talking about. Verbal language is different from culture to culture, however, and so the non-verbal language may also differ. A gesture may have a clear meaning in one culture, but be meaningless or have a completely different meaning in another culture.

b Now read the text. Do your answers agree with the ones in the text? Which of these is closest in meaning to what is said in the text?

1 Body language is the same everywhere.
2 Some body language is the same everywhere.
3 All body language differs from culture to culture.

c Read the text again and find words or phrases that mean:

used by all people   when you're a baby   without meaning

3 Language focus
infinitive of purpose

a Look at these examples:

1 Nodding the head is used *to indicate* 'yes'.
2 A baby turns his head from side to side *to show* he ...

To + infinitive is used to talk about the reason or purpose for doing something. Go back to the text in exercise 2 and find other examples of the infinitive of purpose.

b Finish these sentences.

Example People nod their head to indicate 'yes'.

1 People wear smart clothes to __.
2 Women wear make-up to __.
3 People go to the cinema to __.
4 In my country, people __ to show they're pleased to meet you.
5 In my country, people __ to mean 'goodbye'.

Write two more examples of your own.

4 Personal space

a How do you feel if someone sits or stands very close to you? Why do you feel that way? What do you do?

b Listen to the first part of an interview with Dr Crewe, a body language expert, and answer these questions.

1 What happens if somebody enters your personal space?
2 Who's personal space is larger, Japanese or Americans? Why?

c Now listen to the second part of the radio interview with Dr Crewe and answer these questions:

3 Which three professions does he mention? Why does he mention them?
4 What percentage of a message comes from a) the words? b) tone of voice and body language?
5 Describe what was happening between the Japanese and the American at the conference. Why was it happening?

5 Wordspot
participles as adjectives

a Look at these examples:

1 That's an *amazing* story!
2 I was *amazed* by what he said!

Which example describes the way the speaker is feeling? What does the other example describe?

b Read the sentences and choose the correct form of the word in brackets.

1 Many people are very (*interested/interesting*) in non-verbal communication.
2 I think it's an (*interesting/interested*) subject, myself.
3 I feel very (*frustrated/frustrating*) when I don't understand something.
4 Do you? I just get (*bored/boring*).
5 It's the most (*boring/bored*) book I've ever read.

6 Reading the body

a According to the experts, the body language of the people pictured can tell you how they are feeling and/or what they are thinking. In pairs, decide which of the people in the pictures you think is:

1 frustrated   2 confident   3 bored
4 interested in something   5 making a decision

b Now work with another pair and compare your answers. Were there any you did not agree on?

7 Sayings

a Listen to the woman's response in the three short conversations. She uses the same word in three different ways. For each conversation decide if she is:

1 uncertain   2 bored   3 interested

b Which of the sayings in A is connected with one of the things in B?

A	B
1 Keep your distance.	a facial expression
2 It's not what you said, it's how you said it!	b personal space
3 He gave me such a dirty look.	c tone of voice

c Do you have any similar expressions in your country?

UNIT 2 Rights of the child

1 Saying what you think

a What rights do you think children should have? For example, should they have the right to:
  - say 'no' to medical or dental treatment?
  - appeal if they are suspended or expelled from school?
  - protest if parents or teachers strike them?

b Are there any organisations to protect the rights of children in your country?

2 ActionAid

a ActionAid is a registered British charity. Listen to the tape and answer the questions.

1 When was ActionAid founded?
2 Where does it operate?
3 Who does ActionAid help?
4 How does it help?
5 How can you help?

b What charities are there in your country? In groups, discuss which charities you would support and why.

3 Ademma

a Ademma is one of the children sponsored by ActionAid. Read the project report and answer the questions.

1 How many people does the project help?
2 How is the project trying to solve the problem of illiteracy?
3 How many things does Ademma say she likes/loves doing?
4 What two things does Ademma say she would like to do?
5 Find expressions in the report which are similar in meaning to:
   not enough   poor diet   inability to read and write

b These are the answers to some questions about the text. Write the questions.

Example Going to school.
         What takes up most of Ademma's time?

1 About eleven thousand.
2 6.45 am.
3 A teacher.
4 Dancing.

The Rural Development Trust Project helps about 12,000 families around Anantapur in Southern India. Many of the people in this area are harijans, or social outcasts, which means they are not accepted by Indian society. Their income is insufficient to meet their needs and they face problems like malnutrition, disease and illiteracy. To tackle illiteracy, supplementary schools have been set up in 136 villages and about 11,000 children attend. Parents are taught to understand how important education is to their children's future. Seven-year-old Ademma is one child who attends a supplementary school. Her family owns no land. Both her parents work as farm labourers and Ademma has to help her mother even though going to school takes up most of her day. She says: 'I like going to school. Although I have a long day (starting at 6.45 am and finishing at 6.15 pm) I like learning new things and I love dancing. I would like to be a teacher because I like going to school so much.' Her teacher agrees that dancing is her best subject! Ademma knows about sponsorship and says: 'I don't know my sponsor but I would like to hear from her.'

4 Language focus
gerunds as subjects and objects

a Look at these examples

1 *Going to school* takes up most of her time.
2 I like *going to school*.

b Gerunds are *-ing* words that look like verbs but act like nouns. Because they act like nouns, gerunds can act as (part of) the subject in a sentence, as in sentence 1, or they can act as (part of) the object, as in sentence 2.

Now go back to the text on Ademma and find other examples of gerunds.

c Make a list of five activities you think your partner might enjoy doing. Then ask your partner to find out if you were correct.

Example Student A: Do you like/enjoy cooking?
Student B: Yes, I do./No, I don't. I hate cooking.

5 Wordspot
opposites

a Sometimes prefixes are used to give a word a negative meaning.

in + sufficient = insufficient
im + possible = impossible
il + literate = illiterate
un + kind = unkind

b In pairs, write the opposite of these words using *in-, il-, im-* or *un-*. Use a dictionary to check your answers.

attractive   certain   complete   considerate   correct   educated
legal   logical   patient   perfect   popular   probable   safe

6 Ages of responsibility

a At what age can children in your country legally do or be each of the following?

be convicted of an offence   own a pet   work part-time   leave home (with parental consent)   marry (with parental consent)   leave school   apply for a passport   drink wine in a restaurant   drive   vote   beg on the street

b Now listen to the information on children's rights on a radio programme. Write down the age at which British children can do each of the things listed in part a.

c At what age do you think children should have the rights and responsibilities listed in part a? Are any of the laws in Britain or your country too strict? Not strict enough? Tell the class.

7 Written rights

a Explain in your own words the meanings of these sayings. Do you agree with them? Why?/Why not?

1 Children should be seen and not heard.
2 Charity begins at home.

b In 1959, the United Nations set out a *'Declaration of the Rights of Children'* which set out basic rights for young people. These included the rights to enough food, free education and many others.

In groups, write a similar paper. Say what rights you think children should have. Think about their physical, intellectual and emotional needs.

c When you have finished, read what your group wrote to the class.

UNIT 3

The senses

1 Saying what you think

a Look at the various items in the illustration. Which sense(s) would you use to respond to/appreciate each item?

b Now complete the chart.

Sense organ	eyes				skin
Verb			to smell	to taste	
Sense	vision	hearing	smell	taste	

2 Listening to literature

a Mike teaches English literature. He is blind. Before you listen, in pairs discuss how you think he:
   - 'reads' the books which he teaches to his students.
   - marks essays.

b Now listen to the first part of the interview. Were your suggestions correct?

c Listen to the second half of the interview and answer the questions.

1 According to Mike, how do his students feel at first about the fact that he is blind?
2 When do their feelings start to change?
3 Does he think that disabled and able-bodied people have much contact with one another? Why is this bad for disabled people?
4 What percentage of disabled people don't work?

d Mike says that society is badly designed for disabled people. In what ways is this true/not true in your country?

1 The senses, such as sight or hearing, are essential for ____. All animals and plants are capable of sensing ____ in their environment. A change in light, sound, smell, touch or ____ is known as a stimulus. Most animals have sense organs, such as eyes or ears. The sense organs receive ____, which they pass to the brain by means of nerves. Animals are not all ____ to the same things. Some have a wide range of sense; others rely almost entirely on one sense.

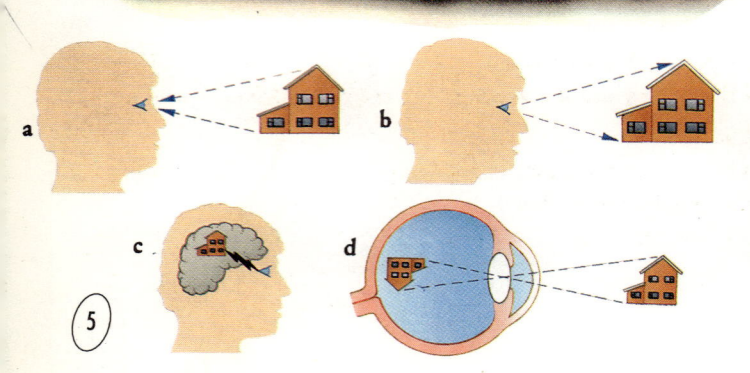

3 Sensitivity

a Which sense gives you the most information? Which sense(s) do you think give(s) the animals in the photos the most information?

b Use these words to complete the first text.

information   sensitive   survival   temperature   changes

c Which two examples of a) senses b) sense organs are mentioned? Which phrase tells you that they are examples?

d Read what the second text has to say about light and vision and put the diagrams in the correct order.

2 Most organisms are sensitive to light, but not all are capable of vision. Vision means using your eyes to form a picture of the world around you. The eyes take in light rays, which are focused by a lens onto light sensitive cells at the back of the eye. The cells send messages to the brain, which interprets them as what you see.

4 Language focus

who and *which* to give extra information

a Look at these examples:

1 Mike teaches English at a college. He is blind.
2 The cells send messages to the brain. The brain interprets the messages as what you see.

The sentences in (1) can be joined with *who* and the sentences in (2) can be joined with *which* to give:

3 Mike, *who* is blind, teaches English at a college.
4 The cells send messages to the brain, *which* interprets them as what you see.

b Non-defining relative clauses are used to give additional information about the person or thing you are talking about. They can occur in the middle or at the end of a sentence. Note the use of commas in the examples. Go back to the texts and find other examples of non-defining relative clauses.

c Match each of the sentences in A with the sentence that follows it in B. Then join the matching sentences using *who* or *which* to replace the word in italics.

A
1 Dogs have strong senses of smell and hearing.
2 Mike uses readers to help him mark his essays.
3 Public transport is not always easy for disabled people to use.
4 Bats use their hearing to catch their prey.

B
a *It* is designed by able-bodied people.
b *They* help them when they are hunting.
c *They* have very large ears.
d *They* are paid by the government.

5 Wordspot

phrasal verbs

a A phrasal verb, eg *see to*, is a verb + adverb and/or preposition that has a single meaning.

> **see to.** If you see to something that needs attention, you attend to it. EG Don't you worry about that. I'll see to that ... A man was there to see to our luggage ...

b Now complete each of these sentences with a phrasal verb beginning with a form of *see*, that has a similar meaning to the word/phrase in brackets.

see about   see off   see through   see to

1 I __ them __ at the airport. (*said goodbye*)
2 I __ him straightaway. (*understood his intentions*)
3 I'll come with to the station to __ your ticket. (*arrange*)
4 I smell burning. I'd better __ the dinner. (*attend to*)

c Now do the same but use phrasal verbs beginning with a form of *look*.

look after   look into   look back

5 I __ on my childhood as a happy time. (*remember*)
6 He __ his younger sisters and brothers for many years. (*took care of*)
7 Don't worry. We'll __ the problem. (*investigate*)

6 I think it's a ...

a Listen to these sounds and write down what you think you hear. Then tell the class.

Example It/That sounds like children playing.
I think it's/that's a ...

b Now look at the inkblot. Tell your partner what you think it looks like.

Example It looks like a ...
I think it's a ...

7 Sayings

Match the words in italics with the phrases.

1 You must *have eyes in the back of your head.*
2 *Hold your tongue.*
3 It *gets right up my nose.*
4 Everything you say to her *goes in one ear and out the other.*

a be quiet
b know everything that's happening
c is forgotten immediately
d annoys me

UNIT 4 Read all about it!

Headlines:
1. Killer dog killed!
2. Warm weather to carry on
3. Tragic death of film star
4. Six killed in motorway accident

a. Temperature hits record high!
b. Actor dies from heart attack
c. Motorway chaos as 6 die in crash
d. Dog put down for causing child's death

1 Saying what you think

a. Find the headlines a - d which match with headlines 1 - 4.
b. Which headlines are more emotional or sensational, and which are more factual? Give reasons for your answers.
c. What newspapers are there in your country? What are the differences between them? Which newspaper do you read?

2 Newspaper styles

a. In Britain people refer to 'popular' and 'serious' newspapers. Popular newspapers tend to use emotional, informal language. Serious newspapers tend to be more factual. Which of the articles do you think comes from a serious newspaper, and which comes from a popular newspaper?
b. Find the information which is the same in both articles. Is this information mainly factual or emotional? Now look at the remaining information in the first article. Is it factual or emotional? Give examples.
c. Why do you think the first article a) has such a long headline? b) includes the picture of the whales?
d. Which article do you think is more interesting? Which one makes you feel more sympathy for the whales? Give your reasons.

3 Radio news

a. Write these newspaper headlines as complete sentences.

   Example Schoolgirl wins £½ million – A schoolgirl has won £½ a million pounds.

   1 Officers discover drug tunnel
   2 Fortune goes to dogs
   3 Kidnappers release millionaire
   4 3 die in blaze

b. Listen to the news broadcasts for the headlines above. Put them into the order in which you hear them on the tape.
c. Now listen to the stories in more detail and complete the sentences below.
   1 John Croft was ___. His kidnappers were paid ___.
   2 Customs officers have discovered ___. It was used for ___.
   3 Three people died last night when ___.
   4 A clerk, John Bailey has left ___. His uncle received ___.
d. In pairs, put the verbs into the correct form, then listen to the last broadcast and check your answers.

   And finally, an eighteen year old schoolgirl (*win*) half a million pounds in a major lottery. Miss Lee (*receive*) her cheque last week at her school where she (*be*) busy with her final exams.

Human chain drags whales from death in sea of blood

Rescuers wade chest deep in water tinged red with the blood of pilot whales as they try to ease the injured creatures back out to sea.

Their huge bodies cut by sharp rocks, 40 whales were stranded in three feet of water after they swam in too close to the beach.

Two of them died from exhaustion after rolling on to the shore at Cheticamp, Nova Scotia.

Canada's Fisheries Department organised the human chain to push the 25 ft whales back out to the open sea and safety.

More than 100 volunteers braved the freezing waters to take part. A corporal with the Royal Canadian Mounted Police, said: "It's hard to say just how successful the operation has been. Only time will tell whether they head out or come back in again. We can only hope."

Bid to save whales

A chain of 100 people struggled at Cheticamp, Nova Scotia, to push about 40 bleeding pilot whales, stranded in three feet of water, back out to sea, Canadian police said.

4 Language focus

present perfect or past simple?

a Look at this example:

An eighteen year old schoolgirl *has won* half a million pounds in a major lottery. Miss Lee *received* her cheque last week …

When we are talking about an event which took place in the recent past but which is still relevant to the present, we use the present perfect. But we use the past simple when we go on to say more about the event, and/or when we place the event in a specific time in the past, eg last night.

b Read the first lines of the news stories that follow and put the verbs in brackets in the past simple or present perfect.

1 The number of unemployed (*drop*) by 1.5 million in under four years, new figures (*show*) yesterday.
2 The Prime Minister (*call*) an early general election for April 20. He (*say*) yesterday that …
3 Actor George Morgan (*die*) in hospital yesterday. He (*be*) 76 and …

5 Wordspot

contents

a Look at the contents list of a newspaper. Which section would you look at to find the following pieces of information?

1 Information about changes in the value of currencies.
2 Details about the life of a famous person who has just died.
3 Readers' opinions of recent articles.
4 A critic's opinion of a recent book.
5 Information about a labour dispute in your own country.
6 Information about an election in another country.

b What other sections might you find in a newspaper? Name at least three.

Inside

Financial news	12-14
Home News	2-5
International News	8-10
Obituary	39
Review	21-24, 28
Letters	31

6 Discussion

a In pairs, discuss which kind of news items you enjoy/do not enjoy reading, like this:

I don't like …   I'm not interested in …   I find … boring.

b In groups, make a list of the sort of things you read for pleasure and for information.

c Now look at your list. As a group decide which of the items on your list you would like to be able to read in English.

7 Improving yourself

a Make a list of ways that you could improve your reading speed and comprehension in English. Then compare with a partner what you have written.

Example Don't look up the meaning of every word I don't understand.

b When would you use this expression? Choose the best answer.

That's news to me!

1 When you are watching the news on television.
2 When someone tells you something you didn't know.

UNIT 5

Young heroes

1 Saying what you think

Which of the following were/are you most concerned about in your teenage years (13 - 19)?

getting good grades at school   your appearance
showing that your parents/teachers were/are wrong
helping other people

What else were/are you concerned about?

Zebrugge girl who saved other lives

Janice was rescued, then went bravely to the rescue herself.

Even though she was lucky to survive the horrific 1987 Herald of Free Enterprise sinking, Janice Parker made sure that she didn't only save herself. Rescued by a tugboat, she helped others by organising bandages, preparing makeshift beds and making coffee. Her noble gestures haven't gone unrewarded - Janice was presented with an award by Dr Pauline Cutting, recently a surgeon in war-torn Beirut. 'But,' says Janice in a very matter-of-fact way, 'it's just an instinct. If people are in a worse position than you, you help them.' And all through it, Janice, now 15, whose father was the man who saved lives by acting as a human bridge, didn't even know whether or not her parents were alive. Later, Dr Cutting said, 'She showed outstanding selflessness, for which I deeply admire her.'

2 Reading

a In 1987, the Herald of Free Enterprise ferry sank in the English Channel. Read the story of one 15-year-old girl, and answer the questions.

1 How was Janice saved?
2 How did she help the other people on the ferry?
3 What is special about her father?
4 What was Janice's reward?

b Find words or phrases in the text that mean the same as:

shocking or horrifying   temporary and of poor quality
a natural way to act

c Janice says: 'It's just an instinct. If people are in a worse position than you, you help them.' Do you think that what Janice did was brave, or do you think that it was something that anyone would have done? Do you think that she deserved an award?

3 Wordspot

synonyms

a Match words in column A with words that are similar in meaning in column B.

A	B
1 brave	a situation
2 rescue	b courageous
3 position	c exceptional
4 outstanding	d save
5 selfless	e unemotional
6 matter-of-fact	f unselfish
7 horrific	g terrible

b Use a form of some of the words from column A to complete the sentences.

1 He's very __ about things; he doesn't often become emotional.
2 He needs help - he's in a very difficult __.
3 He was __ from the sinking ship by the crew from another boat.
4 He's a(n) __ swimmer; he's won several awards.
5 It was a terrible accident - really __.

4 Language focus

adverbs of manner

a Look at this example:

1 They placed *the injured people gently* in the ambulance.

Adverbs of manner usually follow the object or complement.

b Now look at this example:

2 Janice *went bravely* to the rescue.

Adverbs of manner can be placed after the verb when there is no object or complement.

c For each sentence, change the adjective in brackets to an adverb. Then rewrite the sentence to include an adverb. Decide where to place the adverb in the sentence.

Example They waited for someone to help them. *(patient)*
They waited patiently for someone to help them.

1 She worked through the night. *(steady)*
2 She answered their questions. *(honest)*
3 The boat rocked from side to side. *(violent)*
4 She closed the door behind her. *(quiet)*

by + -ing

a Look at this example:

She helped others *by organising* bandages, preparing ...

You can use *by* + *-ing* to describe a method for doing something.

Example How did she help others? By organising bandages ...

b Join these sentences using *by* + *-ing*.

1 Janice's father saved others. He acted as a 'human bridge'.
2 He put out the fire. He poured water on it.
3 He saved her life. He jumped into the water and swam with her to the shore.

5 Youth awards

a Read the text about the Best of British Youth Awards, and answer the questions.

1 What age are the youngest people involved?
2 What have done to deserve an award?
3 What will the winners receive?

b Now listen to a radio broadcast about the six finalists for 1990, and match the names of the finalists with people they have helped below.

people with cancer   physically disabled people   young people in care   mentally disabled people   elderly people
young people who might abuse drugs and alcohol

c Listen again, and write notes about the following for each of the finalists. Then, in pairs, compare your notes.

age   background/experience   how he/she helps/has helped people in need.

What? The Best of British Youth Awards is aimed at young people between the ages of 16 and 21 who are making the most of their own lives and the lives of those around them.
Why? Many young people all over Britain are making a real impact. Some are involved in community work, have started special projects or campaigns, or have overcome a disadvantage in order to make a valuable contribution.
How? Write in and tell us about the achievements of a special young person you know. In doing so you will be giving them the recognition they deserve and the chance to win valuable extra funds for their chosen cause.

6 Discussion

Work in groups. Imagine that you are the judges who have to decide which of the young people in exercise 5 should win first, second and third prizes, then tell the class what your group decided and why.

7 Sayings

Use the expressions below to complete the sentences. You will have to make some changes to the expressions.

put on a brave face   lose one's nerve   keep one's cool

1 I'm afraid. I think I've ___.
2 You'd never know she was so unhappy. She ___.
3 Don't panic ___.

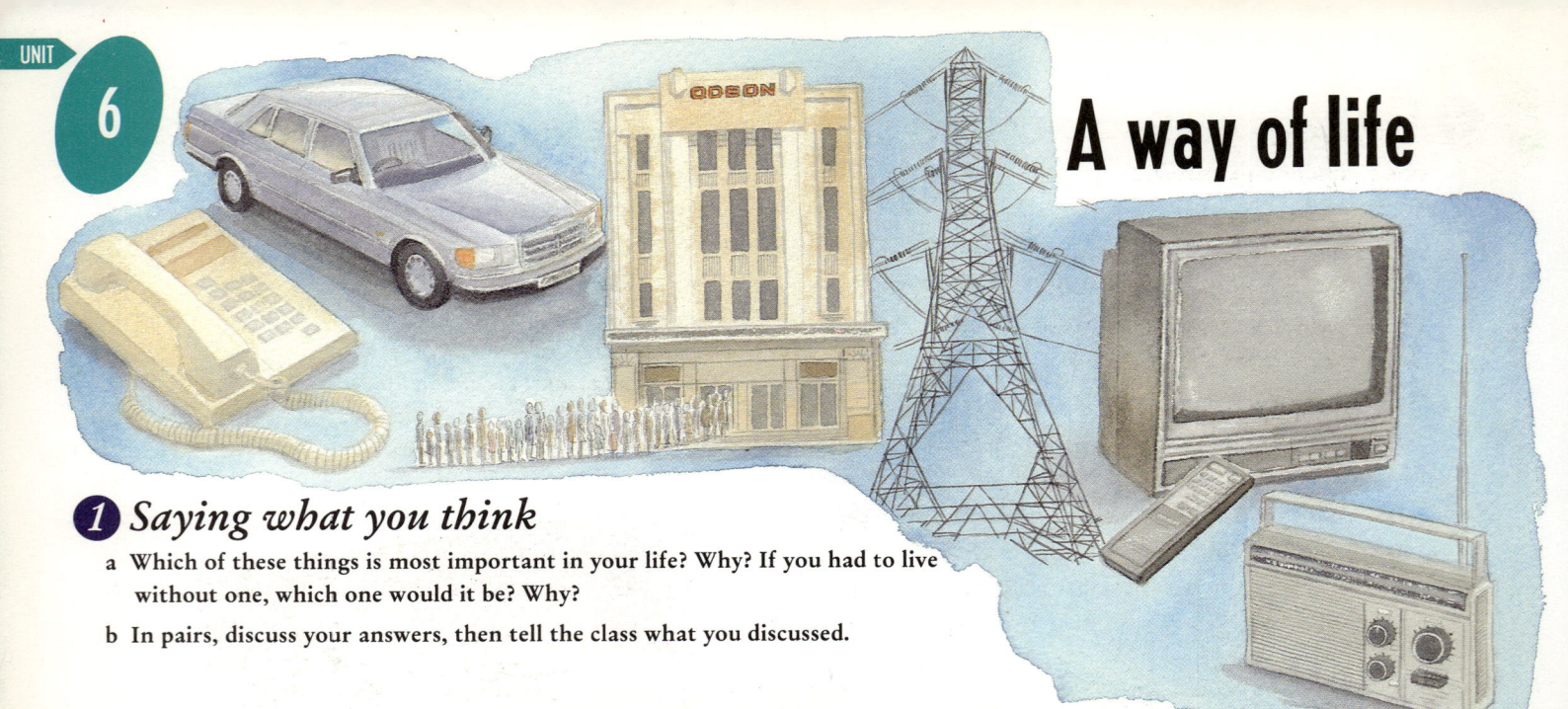

UNIT 6

A way of life

1 Saying what you think

a Which of these things is most important in your life? Why? If you had to live without one, which one would it be? Why?

b In pairs, discuss your answers, then tell the class what you discussed.

2 Holding on to tradition

a Do you think there is anything unusual about the people in the photograph? Write down three things you would like to know about them and their lifestyle.

b Read the text quickly to find out if your questions were answered. Now answer the questions.

1 How long have the Amish lived in America?
2 Why do they live without modern inventions?
3 How do motorists react to the Amish and why?

c Look at the expressions in italics and, in pairs, guess their meaning.

d Mark these statements as true or false and correct the false statements.

1 Unmarried Amish women are supposed to wear black aprons.
2 The Amish are allowed to go to history museums.
3 They are forbidden to go to the theatre.
4 They are discouraged from swimming.
5 They are not supposed to own a camera.
6 They are not allowed to have their photograph taken.

In the farmlands of Lancaster County, Pennsylvania, *time seems to stand still*. Some 2,500 Amish families live there with no other wish than to practise their religion and carry on their lifestyle as they have for over two centuries.

The original Amish *settlers* came to America from Switzerland and Germany around 1720. They trace their *origins* back to a man called Jacob Ammann, and they continue to live as he dictated - close to the land and without modern inventions. Almost every kind of technology is *shunned* - cars, electricity, telephones, radios.

As a result, the old and the modern exist side by side. Busy motorists wait impatiently while bearded Amish men in wide-brimmed felt hats and dark clothing coax their teams of horses to pull black *buggies*. Alongside women in modern fashions, Amish women wear ankle-length dresses, black shawls, black aprons (white if they are single), black cotton stockings and black leather shoes.

The Amish are not allowed to go to the theatre, to the cinema or to amusement parks, although visits to zoos, flower gardens and history museums are not uncommon. They are not supposed to dance or to play cards. All sports except swimming are discouraged. No jewellery may be worn, not even a wedding ring. They are forbidden to own a camera and even *posing* for photographs is discouraged.

3 Your choice

a Would you like to live like the Amish? Why?/Why not?

b The Amish live completely apart from American culture. They speak a different language, educate their children in their own schools, produce their own food and don't vote. Do you think it is right for citizens of a country to live apart from the rest of the society? Do you know of any people like this in your own country?

11

4 Language focus
obligation and permission

a Look at these examples:

1 Married Amish women *are supposed to* wear black aprons.
2 The Amish *are allowed to* go to zoos.

Which of the phrases in italics means a) should / are expected to b) are permitted to?

Now look at these examples:

3 The Amish *are not allowed to* go to the theatre.
4 They *are not supposed to* play cards.

Not allowed to and *not supposed to* in this context have the meaning of *not permitted to*.

b Rewrite the sentences using *(not) supposed to* and *(not) allowed to*.

Example They are forbidden to own a camera.
They are not allowed to own a camera.

1 They are not permitted to dance.
2 Married women are expected to wear black aprons.
3 They are forbidden to wear jewellery.
4 Visits to zoos are not uncommon.

5 Wordspot
phrases

a Look at this example:

The old and the modern exist *side by side*.

Now complete the sentences with similar phrases below.

arm in arm   eye to eye   man to man   word for word

1 We disagree, but then, we don't often see __, do we?
2 The happy young couple walked __ through the town.
3 I want to know exactly what he said. Tell me __.
4 I think that it's time we sat down and talked __.

b Do you know any other expressions like the ones above? Make a list of them and tell the class.

6 It has its ups and downs

a Beth and her husband and two children lived on a houseboat on the River Hamble in Britain from 1950 - 1960. Before you listen to the tape, find out the meanings of these words:

carefree   privacy   gangplank   leak   damp   gale   deck

Listen to part 1 of the interview and answer the questions.

1 Why did they decide to live on a houseboat?
2 Why couldn't they move the boat wherever they wanted?
3 How large was the boat?

b Now listen to part 2 of the interview and note down what Beth says about a) the advantages b) the disadvantages and hardships of living on a houseboat.

c Listen to part 3 and answer the questions.

1 What happened for the first three weeks of August?
2 What happened to them the first time it rained?

d Do you think that Beth enjoyed living on the houseboat? Would you enjoy it? Why?/Why not?

7 Survey

Write three questions to find out how the other students in the class live.

Example Do you have to work long hours?

Ask other students in the class and report back.

UNIT 7

> In villages in Pakistan, a prospective bridegroom is brought before relatives of the bride, who insult him with every known invective. The theory is that, if he can take that, he has nothing to fear from what the bride will say later. *Robin Ray*

> Seven hundred love letters written by a young Taiwanese to his girlfriend have finally brought results. The girl has become engaged to the postman who delivered the letters. *San Francisco Chronicle*

Affairs of the heart

1 Saying what you think

a Look at the two short articles. Do you know any funny stories about love?

b What two qualities do you look for most in a partner?

a sense of humour   faithfulness   honesty   kindness   tolerance   other

c Which qualities would you find least attractive in a partner?

Dear Sarah

Dear Sarah I'm a normal outgoing, confident, 20-year-old guy with a problem! I've been in love with a girl for several months now, but I seem unable to ask her out, as I have no confidence when she's around. This is very unusual for me. I would love to have the courage to approach her, but I'm worried that she will say no. She's very beautiful and is always really nice to me - so what can I do?

Dear Sarah I've been going out with my boyfriend for three years. He is 21 and has been out of work for two of the last three years. I'm sure if he looked for a job he would find one, but he says he's quite happy as he is. I have always thought that the man in my life should have a proper job. What can I do to persuade him to get a job?

Dear Sarah Two years ago, I remarried after being a widow for five years. My husband is a very loving and kind man, but he does not get on with my children. If I invite them to our house, I know he will not accept them, saying that all they want to do is break up our marriage. I know this is not true, but how can I convince him?

2 Agony aunt

a Agony aunts work for a magazine or radio station. People write to them with their problems and they give advice on how to solve those problems.

Read these three letters. Would you use any of these adjectives to describe
a) the writers b) the people mentioned in the letters?

lazy   selfish   loyal   traditional   shy   stubborn   kind   confident

b In groups, choose one of the letters and decide what advice you would give. Tell the class what your group decided.

3 Radio advice

a Now listen to Sarah's advice and match the advice you hear with the person you think the advice is for. Do you disagree with any of the advice?

b Listen to the tape again. Which of these ways of giving advice do you hear?

You must talk to him ...   Try (not) to ...   Why don't you ...   In the end, you must ...
You should/ought to ...   You must ask yourself ...   If you realise ..., (then) accept him ...   If I were you I'd ...   It looks to me like ...   I'd say ...   Just talk to her ...

13

4 Wordspot
synonyms and antonyms

a Find words or phrases in the letters in exercise 2 that are similar in meaning (synonyms) to these:

   afraid   destroy   man   persuade   sociable

b Now find words or phrases that mean the opposite (antonyms) of:

   cruel   employed   normal   shy

5 Language focus
first and second conditional

a Look at these examples:

1 If I invite them to our house, I know he will not accept them *(and I might invite them)*.
2 If he looked for a job, I know he would find one *(but I know he doesn't want one)*.

In which of the examples is the speaker referring to:

a) a future event which she thinks is likely? (first conditional)
b) a future event which she thinks is possible but not likely to happen? (second conditional)

b Find the verbs in the examples above. What tenses are they in? Why are these tenses used?

c Complete these sentences. Decide if you need to use the first or the second conditional.

1 If I win/won a foreign holiday, I'll/I'd …
2 If I am/was invited out to dinner this evening …
3 If I find/found some money in the street …
4 If this lesson finishes/finished early …

6 Personal replies

a In pairs, write a letter of advice to one of the people in exercise 2. When you have finished, exchange letters with another pair and make corrections.

b In groups, discuss why you think people write to agony aunts. Make a list of your reasons and then compare it with another group's list. Would you ever write a letter like this?

7 Perfect partners

Look at the words and phrases for describing people. Put them under the following headings: *Looks, Character, Interests* and *Career.* Then choose two words from each column and write about your perfect partner.

honest   accountant   caring   romantic   good-looking   sincere   sense of humour   horse riding   bank manager   country walks   romantic dinners   attractive   intelligent   doctor   plump   independent   career-minded   non-smoker   travel   wine tasting   fashion model   pretty   clean-shaven

UNIT 8
The language of colour

1 Saying what you think

Colours have different meanings in different cultures. In groups, talk about what associations colours have for you. Think about:

marriage   death   sadness   illness   danger   happiness   politics   other

2 Science and colour

a Read the first paragraph of the text about scientist Isaac Newton and answer the questions.

1 Was Newton looking for information about colour when he made his discovery?
2 What did people think about colour before Newton made his discovery?
3 What did Newton prove instead?

b Now read the second paragraph. Some words are illegible. Decide which words below fit where in the text.

beam   experiment   prism   rays   source   spectrum

Man's understanding of colour results mainly from the work of Isaac Newton in the seventeenth century. While he was investigating ways to improve the telescope, Newton made a discovery which completely changed man's understanding of colour. Before Newton's discovery, people thought that a colour was contained within the object. Newton proved that this was not true. He showed that colour is created by light falling upon the object. Newton showed that light is the source of colour.

Newton's experiment was done in a darkened room. First, Newton passed a beam of light through a glass prism. When it emerged from the prism, the light was no longer a single beam of white light. It had become the spectrum of the seven rays of colour - red, orange, yellow, green, blue, indigo and violet. In the second stage of his experiment, Newton placed a second prism in the path of the light, but the light which emerged from the second prism was no longer a colour spectrum. It was a single beam of light. Newton had found the source of colour - light.

3 Colour in your life

a What does colour mean in your life? Note down a colour which you associate with each of the following:

1 energy / aggression   2 cheerfulness / interest in other people
3 self-confidence / optimism   4 nature / tradition   5 peace / sadness

b Now listen to June Fox, a colour consultant, talking about the effects of colour, and answer the questions.

1 What two things does she say colour affects?
2 What does she advise people about?
3 What colours does she associate with the words in part a?

How far do you agree with what she said?

c Look at the rooms. Which ones would you like/not like to be in? Why? How would the colours in each room make you feel? In pairs, choose one of the rooms and say how you would improve the colours in it.

4 Language focus
pronouns in defining relative clauses

a Defining relative clauses define or explain which person or thing you are talking about. Look at this example. Which noun does the clause in italics define/explain?

Newton made a discovery *which/that completely changed man's understanding of colour.*

b When the relative pronoun *which* or *who*, is the subject of a defining relative clause, you can replace it with *that*. When the relative pronoun, *who, which* or *that* is the object of a defining relative clause, it can be omitted entirely.

Yellow is a nice, sunny colour. Many people like *it*.
Yellow is a nice, sunny colour (*which/that*) many people like.

c Now join these sentences using a relative pronoun.

Example This is the room. I slept in *it* when I was a child.
This is the room *which/that* I slept in when I was a child.

1 Newton was the scientist. *He* discovered that light is the source of colour.
2 Red is a colour. *It* can make you appear aggressive if you wear too much.
3 Yellow is a colour. I wear *it* when I'm feeling confident.
4 In hot countries, people paint their rooms in colours. *These colours* reflect the sunlight and cool the room.

d In which of the statements in part c could you leave out the relative pronoun?

5 Wordspot
word set

a Match the words in A with the colours in B to make compound words describing colours.

A blood snow royal iron jet lime nut
B grey blue red black green brown white

b In pairs, decide which colours suit/don't suit you. Which colours would clash with what you are wearing and which colours would match?

6 Survey

Choose one of the questions below and ask at least three other people in the class.

1 What is your favourite colour and what does it remind you of?
2 Which colour do you like the least and what does it make you think of?
3 Which colours do you wear the most/the least often and why?
4 Have you always liked/disliked the same colours, or have your colour preferences changed?
5 Which colour(s) would you paint any one of these rooms in your house and why: your bedroom, a kitchen, a study, a living room?

7 Colour chart

a Which word could complete all three sentences? In each sentence, the underlined word or phrase means the same as the word or phrase in brackets.

1 He passed his exams with flying ...s. (*very successfully*)
2 Anger ...ed his judgement. (*affected*)
3 He told a very ...ful story. (*full of exciting details*)

b In pairs, choose a colour from the chart, but do not tell your partner what colour you have chosen. *Student A*: Ask five questions to find out what colour your partner has chosen. *Student B*: Answer only yes or no.

Example Is it a deep/dark/bright/pale/ shade of red?
Is it number 3?
Is it lighter/darker/brighter than number 3?

1 2 3 4 5 6 7 8 9 10

UNIT 9
Service with a smile?

1 Saying what you think

a Where do you expect to find service? In pairs, discuss which of the following you associate with good service:

careful attention   speed   good value   politeness
efficiency   efficient response to complaints

b In your country, are people in shops and restaurants generally polite and helpful? How do standards of service in your country compare with standards of service in other countries that you have been to? Tell the class.

1 10 DAYS TOURING Enjoy Europe's wonderful scenery, passing deep blue lakes with pretty towns and villages set against a backdrop of majestic snow-capped mountains. Sit back, relax and enjoy the peaceful pace of life as you make your way through the beautiful countryside in our fully equipped coach by day, and live it up at night in a fashionable, modern hotel ...

2 Enjoy **14 DAYS** of peace, quiet and relaxation at one of our biggest and best-known family resorts. Sandy beaches, lush palm trees and lots of sun. Travel to the continent with one of our experienced coach drivers on our fully equipped coach. Our clean, beautifully designed and private apartments are located near the beach in an idyllic family resort with fine panoramic views. Facilities include: a large swimming pool and pool bar and a children's pool.

3 THE PARK HOTEL is a luxury five star hotel situated on its own beach. Accommodation is in air-conditioned bedrooms all with balcony, bathroom, telephone, TV and video. The superb facilities include: shops, a health club and two swimming pools. For entertainment there are theme evenings and a resident orchestra.

2 Holiday upset

a In pairs, discuss what sort of things could ruin a holiday for you. Look at the advertisements for holidays. What sort of things could go wrong?

b Now listen to Anne Wright talking about her family's holiday. Which of the holidays did they take? Did they enjoy it? What is Mrs Wright going to do next?

c Here is part of the complaints form that Mrs Wright sent to the holiday company. Listen to the tape again and complete the form.

CUSTOMER SERVICE FORM
Complaint:
1 ... was not experienced and got lost.
2 ... broke down because it hadn't been checked properly before we left.
3 ... had been put on the wrong coach.
4 ... was filthy and even when I complained to the representatives, it wasn't cleaned.
5 It was impossible to close the ..., so we had no privacy.
6 ... had not been filled.
7 ... and ... that were described in the brochure did not exist.
8 ... played loud music all day long and it was impossible to get any peace.

3 Wordspot
homonyms

a Many words in English have more than one meaning. *Bar* as it is used in exercise 2 means a place where you can buy a drink. What other meanings of *bar* can you find in the dictionary? Tell the class.

b Choose from these words to complete the sentences.

bar   club   coach   form   resort

1 You should never __ to violence - there is always another way to solve a problem.
2 Air travel is a popular __ of transport with many businessmen.
3 Would you hand me my golf __, please?
4 I'm in love with my tennis __ .
5 Would you like a __ of chocolate?

c What is the meaning of the words above when they are used to talk about holidays?

4 Language focus

passive

a Look at these examples:

1 The apartment *wasn't cleaned up*.
2 The food and drink *had been put* on the wrong coach.

Go back to the complaints form in exercise 2 and find other examples of the passive.

You use the passive a) when you want to stress the action itself, and/or b) because the agent or doer of the action is obvious and needs no special attention.

When the agent is important to the meaning of the sentence, you can use *by* + agent.

3 Promises were made *by the representatives*.

b Now write these sentences in the passive. You should use *by* + agent in one of statements 1 - 4. Why?

Example The holiday company ruined the Wright's holiday.
The Wright's holiday was ruined by the holiday company.

1 They had promised the Wrights food and drink on the coach, and there was none.
2 No one had checked the coach properly before they set off.
3 The representatives ignored the Wrights' complaints.
4 They didn't clean the room even though Mrs Wright complained.

5 Consumer rights

a Listen to the two short conversations. What does each person want to return? Why?

b These are some of the things that you can do if a product is faulty, or if you are not happy with it.

1 Return the item and:
  - demand a refund.
  - accept a credit note.
2 Exchange the item.
3 Take it back to be repaired.
4 Ask for a discount.
5 Keep the item and:
  - do nothing.
  - see a solicitor.

Now listen again. Which course of action do you think each customer should take? In your country, what would your legal rights be in the situations on the tape?

c Now listen to a radio phone-in programme. What course of action does Clare Morgan advise the customers in part a to do?

6 Roleplay

In pairs, practise this situation. Take turns at being the customer and manager.

Student A: You are in a restaurant. The waiter has brought you the fish that you ordered, but you don't think that it is fresh. Complain to Student B (the manager) and ask for your money back.

Student B: You are the manager of the restaurant. You know that the fish was caught this morning. You don't want to refund Student A.

7 Service signs

a In pairs, suggest possible endings for this well-known saying.

The customer is always ...

Are there any similar expressions in your language?

b Where would you expect to see the signs pictured? What does each of them mean?

UNIT 10

Men and women

1 Saying what you think

Which of the following do you think best describe men, women, or men and women equally?

good at mechanics   good at maths   good at languages   good judges of character   decisive   aggressive   intuitive   compassionate   sensitive   artistic   good judges of space and distance

Compare and discuss your answers with a partner, and then tell the class.

---

1 You hear the faint meow of a cat. How easily can you place the cat without looking round?
a You can point straight to it.
b If you think about it, you can point straight to it.
c You don't know if you could point to it.

2 How good are you at remembering a song you've just heard?
a You find it easy and you can sing part of it in tune.
b You can only do it if it's a simple, rhythmical song.
c You find it difficult.

3 A person you've met a few times telephones you. Could you easily tell whose voice it was in the first few seconds?
a You'd find it quite easy.
b You'd recognise the voice more than half the time.
c You'd recognise the voice less than half the time.

4 In your early school days, how easy did you find spelling and the writing of essays?
a Both were quite easy.
b One was easy.
c Neither was easy.

5 You see a place to park your car, but you must back into it and it's a fairly small space. What do you do?
a You look for another space.
b You back into it ... carefully.
c You back into it without much thought.

6 You've spent three days in a strange village and someone asks you which way is north.
a You're unlikely to know.
b You're not sure, but given a moment you can work it out.
c You point north.

7 You're in a dentist's waiting room with several people of the same sex. How close can you sit to one of them without feeling uncomfortable?
a Less than 15 cm.
b 15 cm to 60 cm.
c Over 60 cm.

2 Point of difference

a *Brainsex* is a controversial new book that argues that men and women think and behave differently because their brains are different. The quiz was written to test if a person had a 'male' or a 'female' brain. Read the quiz and check that you understand all the vocabulary.

b Listen to a man being asked the questions from the quiz, and note down his answers.

c Now do the quiz yourself. Check your score with the teacher.

3 Boys and girls

a When you were a child, which of the following were you allowed or expected to do?

(not) cry if you were hurt   be good at sports   learn to cook   learn to fight   look after younger children

b In groups, compare the ways in which the men and women in the group were brought up. Think about toys you played with, colours you wore, games you played, how your parents/teachers expected you to behave.

c Now tell the class what your group discussed and say why you think there are differences.

4 Wordspot
suffixes

a These adjectives describe people. Change them into nouns. Sometimes, more than one noun is possible.

aggressive   comfortable   compassionate   decisive   intelligent   intuitive   sensitive

b Look at the words above. Which of these suffixes do you associate with adjectives, and which with nouns: -ive, -ion, -ness, -ity, -able?

5 Language focus
because and *because of*

a You use *because (of)* to express cause or reason.

Look at these examples:

1 Men and women behave differently *because their brains are different.*
2 Men and women behave differently *because of differences in their brains.*

Because is followed by a clause. **Because of** is followed by a noun or noun phrase, and is more formal

b For each of these sentences, use the word in brackets to give a reason for the action or event. Finish each sentence using *because* and *because of*.

Example He gets into fights because __. (aggressive)
            He gets into fights because he's aggressive.
            because of his aggressiveness.

1 She does well at school because __. (intelligent)
2 He got the job of Departmental Manager because __. (decisive)
3 She prefers to live in a warm climate because __ to the cold. (sensitive)

make

a Look at this example from the tape:

Sitting too close to someone *makes me (feel) very uncomfortable.*

In this sentence, *make* has the meaning of cause.

b Now ask your partner what makes him/her feel:

angry   happy   nervous   proud   sad   *frightened*

Example What makes you (feel) angry?
            Waiting in traffic jams makes me very angry.

6 Discussion

a Say how strongly you agree/disagree with these statements:

1 Men and women are not equal - men/women are naturally superior to women/men.
2 Men and women are equal but not the same because they are taught from childhood to behave differently from one another.
3 Men and women think and behave differently because their brains are different.

b Discuss your opinions in groups. Then tell the class what you decided giving reasons for your decision.

7 Lateral thinking

In pairs, work out the answer to the puzzle.

A man was taking his son to school one morning. Suddenly, a lorry appeared from the opposite direction. The father braked, but it was too late. The lorry crashed headlong into the front of the car, killing the father. The badly injured boy was rushed to hospital in an ambulance. As he was being taken into casualty on a stretcher, the doctor who was hurrying to help him suddenly stopped, turned very pale, and said, 'Oh, no! That's my son!' Who is the doctor?

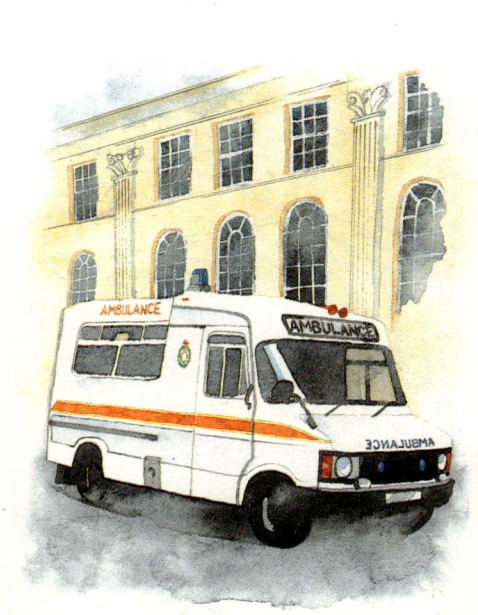

UNIT 11

Ceremonies and festivals

1 Saying what you think

a What ceremonies or festivals are represented in the pictures?

b When do people get together and celebrate in your country? Think about:
- ceremonies, eg weddings
- festivals, eg religious celebrations

c Which of the ceremonies and festivals above mark an important turning point or stage in life; a historical or religious event; a seasonal event?

2 An important ceremony

a Read the text about an important ceremony on the island of Bali in Indonesia and answer the questions.

1 What do the Balinese have done to their teeth?
2 Why do they have it done?

b Find words or phrases in the text that are similar in meaning to:

adolescence   not straight or even   an important responsibility
arrives   the dead person   look like   reaching

c Read the text again and find the answers to these questions:

1 What do the Balinese people not want to look like? Why not?
2 What do unfiled teeth look like to the Balinese?
3 According to the text, tooth filing can be done at various times in a person's life. When should it be done? At what other times can it be done?
4 Why must a person's teeth be filed before he/she is buried or cremated?

d In pairs, discuss what people do or have done in your country at these times. Choose one event and then tell the class.

when you get married	when a child is born
when someone dies	when you get engaged
when you start school	when you reach the age of majority

The Balinese people have a horror of looking in any way like an animal, and shortly after puberty, both boys and girls should have their teeth filed. Because pointed, long and irregular teeth are associated with animals, the filing of the teeth is an essential duty. The object is to produce flat, even teeth, in other words, the opposite of the curved, pointed fang. If teeth filing is not performed at puberty, it is often combined with the marriage ceremony, thus combining two ceremonies into one. In a family that has had recent good luck, a tooth filing with invited guests may be arranged for a group of adolescents and young adults. But when the expert turns up, various middle-aged or old men and women will suddenly remember that they have never had it done, and decide to have their teeth filed by the expert. If by any chance a Balinese has not had his teeth filed before he dies, his relatives must ensure that it is done before he is buried or cremated. Otherwise, the deceased will resemble an animal and will have no chance of attaining heaven.

3 Wordspot
word set

a Decide which of these words are to do with humans and which are to do with animals.

beak   claw   fang   fur   hair   hand   hide   mouth   nail   nose   paw   skin   snout   tooth

b Now write the human and animal equivalents together.

Example tooth (human) - fang (animal)

4 Language focus
have something done

a Look at this example:

Shortly after puberty, both boys and girls should *have their teeth filed*.

Who does the filing a) the boys and girls? or b) someone else?

Now go back to the text and find similar examples of *have something done*.

b Which of the following do you do yourself and which do you have done? Discuss in pairs.

car repair   hair/cut   eyes/test   house/clean   clothes/iron
house/decorate   nails/file   cut/grass   teeth/checked

Example Do you have your car repaired? - Yes I do./No, I don't. I repair it myself.
Who repairs it? - A mechanic.

5 A festival

a What do you know about Chinese New Year and how it is celebrated? In pairs, discuss the answers to these questions.

1 When does Chinese New Year take place?
2 Why do people celebrate it?
3 How do they prepare for it?
4 How do people celebrate the New Year?

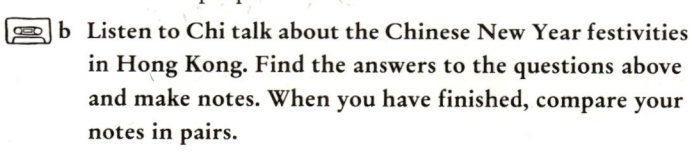

b Listen to Chi talk about the Chinese New Year festivities in Hong Kong. Find the answers to the questions above and make notes. When you have finished, compare your notes in pairs.

6 A talk

Prepare a short talk to give to your class, describing a festival or special occasion in your country. Include:

The background to the event:
- when it takes place.
- why people celebrate it.

The preparation for the event:
- what people do/have done.

The celebration of the event:
- what people wear, do, eat.

7 Greetings

a What do you say in these situations?

1 Someone tells you it's his/her birthday.
2 Someone tells you he/she is engaged to be married.
3 You are in Britain and it's the first of January.

b Find out the dates of the following events this year.

1 Christmas Day
2 Boxing Day
3 Chinese New Year
4 Easter
5 First day of Ramadan
6 Passover

Which of these events take place on the same day every year?

UNIT 12

The universe beyond

1 Saying what you think

a What are the names of the figures in the photographs? Which of them is
   a) a planet b) a galaxy c) a constellation?

b The United States, Russia and other countries have spent huge amounts of money exploring space. In pairs, say which of these two quotes you most agree with and why.

1 Space exploration is a waste of time and money. We should solve our problems here on earth before we go wasting money on space programmes.
2 We live on a shrinking planet. Space programmes may be necessary for mankind to survive.

Back in space, but doubts remain.

1   NASA has come back from the dark days following the Challenger disaster in January 1986. After months of doubt and delays, a new space shuttle, the Discovery, went into space in September 1988. Its four-day mission was a complete success.

2   There is much disagreement on what, exactly, NASA's goals should be. Samuel Phillips, former head of the Apollo programme favours an ambitious approach: 'I'd like to see it lead to planetary exploration with humans. That's a long-term goal.'

3   Other voices are not so confident that space is where humans should be. One newspaper has said that the manned space programme should be abandoned unless it can produce some useful goals. It said: 'Almost all the advantages of space exploration come from unmanned rockets and automatic spacecraft. Putting humans in space multiplies cost and risk.'

4   At the moment, NASA still plans to build a manned space station some time in the mid-nineties. This will be used to develop new materials in a low-gravity environment and to test the effects of long-term space flight on humans. Other ideas include sending a manned expedition to the Martian moon by the year 2000, and putting an observatory on the dark side of the moon by 2004.

5   NASA's future does not depend on NASA alone. It depends mostly on Congress and the President. The US President has backed the space programme. He will be asked to do more - to set America's space policy for years to come. America has returned to space, but where in space should it go and how should it get there?

2 Back in space

a These are the topics of the five paragraphs of the text. Read the article about the United States space programme and choose the right topic for each paragraph.

a An argument against manned space flights.
b NASA's plans for the future.
c What NASA's goals should be.
d The future for NASA.
e The launch of the new space shuttle.

b Read the text again in more detail and find the answers to the questions.

1 When did the Discovery space shuttle go into space? Why was it 'after months of doubt and delays'?
2 Who is Samuel Phillips? What long-term goal does he favour?
3 What is the argument against manned space flights?
4 What does NASA plan to have done a) by 1999 b) by 2001 c) by 2005?

c Invent your own name for a space shuttle. What other types of shuttles can you think of?
How would you answer the last question in the text?

3 Wordspot
vocabulary in context

Find words or phrases in the text that are similar in meaning to these phrases.

Example the exploration of other planets
          planetary exploration

1 programme that sends men into space
2 increases greatly
3 travelling/being in space for a long period of time
4 a special building used to study space
5 has given his support to

4 Language focus
future perfect

a Look at this example:

By 2005, NASA *will have built* an observatory on the dark side of the moon.

Have NASA built the observatory yet? Do we know when they intend to build it?

b You use the future perfect *(will have done)* to describe an action or event that a) has not yet happened, and b) will happen before a specified time in the future.

c In pairs, ask and answer questions about what you think will have happened by the 21st century. Use these notes:

- find/a cure for cancer
- find/a cure for AIDS
- discover/a way to stop people ageing
- stop/exploring space

Example Do you think they will have found a cure for cancer by the next century?

Yes, I think so./No, I don't think so./I don't know.

d Complete the following sentences about yourself.

1 When I finish this English course, I will have ...
2 Within the next five years, I hope I will have ...

5 Space travel

a You are going to listen to a radio discussion with Dr Green about space exploration. Before you listen, find the meanings of the following:

resources   colonies   industries   metals   wars   fought

b Listen to the discussion and answer the questions.

1 What are the arguments against space travel?
2 According to Dr Green, why are people on Earth starving?
3 Dr Green says that space exploration could give mankind 'the opportunity to move away from earth'. What examples does he give?
4 How will space shuttles change our lives?

c Which of Dr Green's predictions do you agree/disagree with?

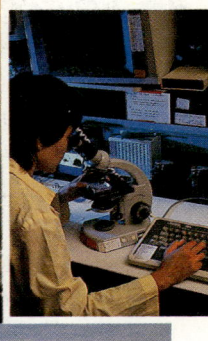

6 Discussion

a Imagine you have a lot of money to spend on these things:

1 cleaning up the environment
2 space exploration
3 medical research
4 improving conditions for poor and hungry people

In groups, put them in order of importance. Write down three reasons for your first choice and three reasons for your last choice.

b Show the class what your group wrote while you tell the class about your choices and explain your reasons for them.

c As a class, decide which group gave the best reasons for their decisions.

7 Space quiz

Find the answers to these questions about space.

1 What is the name of the fifth planet in our solar system?
2 What do you call a group of stars that appear to make a pattern in the sky?
3 Which two planets in our solar system have rings around them?
4 The sun is mainly made up of which gas?
5 Who said: 'One small step for man; one giant step for mankind', and when did he say it?

UNIT 13
Success and failure

In 1963, Ronnie Biggs and several other men, robbed a train of £2,631,784. Ronnie Biggs escaped with the money to South America, where he is still living in luxury.

Mozart, one of the greatest musical composers of all time, died in poverty aged 35

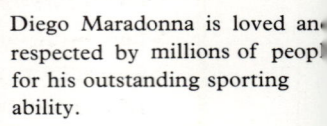

Diego Maradonna is loved and respected by millions of people for his outstanding sporting ability.

1 Saying what you think

a In groups, decide how you would finish this definition, then tell the class giving reasons for your choice.

A successful person is someone who:
- has a lot of money.
- has an important or powerful job.
- is happy.
- is loved and respected by other people.
- does his/her job to the best of his/her ability.

b Who is the most/least successful person you know? Describe him/her to the class.

---

a His disguise kept customers and employers from seeing his face - but it also kept him from seeing them. He stumbled around the bank for a while, and then decided it was time to get on with the job.

b Wishing to help, Mr Pike told them he spoke some French and offered to assist them. He rushed them to the Gare du Nord, asked at the desk for a ticket to Boulogne, dashed down Platform 6 and got the family from Sheffield on board the train.

c Colin Rich, twenty-seven and unemployed, tried to live up to his name, but it just wasn't his day. His first mistake was putting on three stocking masks and a scarf as he entered a London, Ontario bank that he intended to rob.

d It was only as he was walking back down the platform that he looked at the noticeboard and realised that he had put the family on a train for Bologna in Italy, a country with whose language and ways they were even less familiar.

e He reached into his pocket for a gun, and pulled out a glasses case instead. When caught by the police, he was hiding behind a car outside the bank.

(1) f In 1978, Mr Hugh Pike rushed to the aid of a British family in distress. Their car had broken down in Bordeaux and they needed a spare part from Britain so they had to abandon the vehicle. They spoke no French. They couldn't get back to Boulogne to catch the boat. It was now Sunday night and the father had to be at work in Sheffield at 8.00 the next morning.

2 How to succeed

a Listen to three speakers from different countries giving their opinions on what it takes to be successful in their country. Which of the following points does each person mention and in what order?

ambition   good education   hard work
having a wealthy family   knowing the right people
natural ability   well-educated parents

b Which two of the factors above do none of the people mention? Which factor do two of the speakers think is the most important?

3 Disaster time

a The paragraphs from two stories have been jumbled up. In pairs, put the paragraphs for each story into the correct order.

b What happened to the British family and to Colin Rich? In pairs, each student should take one of the stories and retell it in his/her own words.

c If Mr Pike hadn't rescued the family, what do you think they would have done? If Colin Rich hadn't worn so many masks, what do you think might have happened?

4 Language focus
third conditional

a Look at these examples:

1 The family's car broke down, so they didn't catch their train.
2 Their car needed a spare part from Britain, so they abandoned it.

These situations can be rewritten as:

3 If their car hadn't broken down, they would have caught their train.
4 If their car hadn't needed a spare part from Britain, they wouldn't have abandoned it.

Find the verbs in 3 and 4. What tense are they in?

When you are talking about something that might have happened in the past, but didn't happen, you can use the third conditional.

b Rewrite these situations as sentences in the third conditional.

Example Mr Pike offered to help the family, so they got on the train to Italy. - If he hadn't offered to help the family, they would not have got on the train to Italy.

1 The family couldn't speak French, so they couldn't get help from a French person.
2 Mr Pike didn't speak French well, so he put the family on the wrong train.
3 He didn't check the noticeboard, so he put the family on the wrong train.

c Now write sentences about Colin Rich, using sentences in the third conditional.

5 Wordspot
related words

a Look at these examples:

1 Their *car* had broken down ... so they had to abandon the *vehicle*.
2 Wishing to *help*, Mr Pike ... offered to *assist*.

How are the words in italic in each sentence related?

b Now find the words and phrases that are equivalent in meaning in these sentences:

1 English was the only language the family spoke.
2 They didn't want to abandon their car, but it had broken down and they had to leave it.
3 Mr Pike rushed to the station and dashed down platform 6.
4 He reached into his pocket for a weapon and pulled out a gun

6 Survey

a What do you think it takes to be successful? In pairs, add other factors to the list in exercise 2. Then put the factors in order of importance.

b Ask other pairs what they think are the three most important items in the list, and why. Make notes so that you can tell the class what you found out.

c What is/was your greatest success or your biggest failure? Tell the class.

7 Success or failure?

a Finish these headlines with the words *success* or *failure*. In one of the headlines, you could use either word.

b Find out about the life of someone you think was a great success, and write a few paragraphs about him/her.

1 ... story

2 Project doomed to ...

3 Overnight ...

4 Exam ... rate doubles

5 Power ... throws city into darkness

UNIT 14

Future memory?

1 Saying what you think

a Do you remember your dreams? Do you ever dream in colour?

b How important are your dreams? Read these three statements about dreams. Do you agree with any of them?

1 Everyone has dreams that predict future events, but not everyone remembers them.
2 Dreams are the mind's way of working through problems that occur during the day. They can help us to find solutions.
3 Dreams are the rubbish of the mind. They are not significant.

2 A good night's sleep

a What are the facts about dreams? Read the questions below. For each question decide which of the alternatives in brackets you think is the correct answer.

1 What proportion of our lives do we spend asleep? (one fifth/one quarter/one third)
2 How many times do we dream each night? (1 or 2, 4 or 5, 9 or 10)
3 How long do dreams last? (a few seconds/a few seconds to half an hour/an hour or more)
4 Who spends the least time dreaming? (babies/children/adults)
5 Who spends the most time dreaming? (snakes/rabbits/cats)
6 What happens to animals that are prevented from dreaming? (They learn to sleep without dreaming./They become very aggressive./They die.)

b Now listen to Dr Roberts, a scientist who has studied dreams. Use the information on the tape to check your answers to the questions in part a.

3 Language focus

direct and indirect speech

a Which of these statements is direct speech and which is indirect speech?

1 Dr Roberts said, 'Studies have shown that dreams decrease with age.'
2 Dr Roberts said that studies had shown that dreams decrease with age.

b When sentences are changed from direct to indirect speech, how do these verbs usually change?

do   did   is doing   has done   will   can

c Look at these sentences in direct speech and indirect speech:

1 Dr Roberts said, 'We spend one third of our lives asleep.'
2 Dr Roberts said (that) we *spend/spent* one third of our lives asleep.

In sentence 2, you can use either the present or past tense because the situation is still true.

3 Dr Roberts said, 'In recent experiments, scientists prevented people from dreaming.'
4 Dr Roberts said (that) in recent experiments, scientists *prevented/had prevented* people from dreaming.

In sentence 4 you can use either the past perfect or the past simple without changing the meaning.

d Put these statements into indirect speech. Begin with *He said that ...*

1 'Scientists are studying the importance of dreams.'
2 'They have done sleep experiments with animals.'
3 'A few animals died in the experiments.'
4 'All mammals dream.'
5 'I'll be happy to answer any questions.'

4 Wordspot
reporting verbs

a Look at these examples:

1 'I think you're right,' he *agreed*.
2 'Put that down,' he *yelled*.

Which of the reporting verbs in italics describes a) the purpose of what was said? b) the way in which it was said?

b Choose the most appropriate verb to complete the sentences.

admitted cried promised replied suggested whispered

1 'Let go! You're hurting me!' she ___.
2 'It was my mistake,' he ___.
3 'Let's go for dinner,' he ___.
4 'Don't tell anyone - it's a secret,' she ___.
5 'I won't forget,' she ___.
6 'Good afternoon.' 'Good afternoon,' he ___.

c What other verbs do you know that can be used instead of *said* in direct speech?

5 Dream talk

a Is there a language of dreams? If so, how well do you understand it? In pairs, match these common dreams with what they are said to mean.

Dream	Significance
1 house	a fear of not achieving a goal.
2 water	b desire, ambition, emotion, healing.
3 falling	c birth
4 flying	d the end of a phase in life.
5 death	e your body, mind and spirit.
6 teeth	f your emotions.
7 snakes	g stages in your life.
8 a star	h ability to rise above worldly problems.
9 being in a tunnel	i the present is difficult, but there is hope for the future.

b Do you agree with the meanings above? Are there any meanings you can suggest that are not given?

c Read about one man's dream. In pairs, decide what the dream means or is trying to tell the man.

> 'I am standing in a garden outside a house. The garden is overgrown and the outside of the house is a mess: the paint is peeling, and the windows look dull and dirty. But inside the house, I find it is neat, clean and tidy. And there is a meal in the kitchen waiting for me.'

6 A dream come true?

a Listen to a woman telling the story of a dream that she had, and answer the questions.

1 What did she lose?
2 Why couldn't she replace it immediately?
3 What happened in her dream?
4 What happened shortly after she had her dream?

b How would you explain what happened to the woman?

c In pairs, discuss whether you, or anyone you know has ever experienced any of the following.

A dream that predicted a future event.
A strange coincidence.
A premonition, for example when the phone rings and you know who it is before you answer it.
Any other experience that is strange or that you can't explain in the normal way.

7 Sayings

Which of the words below is closest in meaning to the word or phrase in italics in each of the sentences?

desire imagine ideal invent consider

1 I can't believe it! I've just found my *dream* house.
2 Put your money away. I wouldn't *dream of* letting you pay for the meal.
3 How did you *dream up* an idea like that?
4 I never *dreamed* something like this would happen.
5 My greatest *dream* is to visit New Zealand.

UNIT 15

Intentions and regrets

1 Saying what you think

a Match the words describing stages of development with the photographs.

teenager toddler infant adult child

About what age is the person in each of the photos?

b What is your earliest memory? Why do you think you remember it?

2 No regrets

a Listen to Helen talking about her youth and choose the correct answer.

1 At first, Helen was going to become a) a gymnastics teacher b) a professional athlete c) an assistant in a sports shop.
2 Instead, she became a) a nurse b) a secretary c) a nanny.
3 What are her feelings now? a) She wishes she had become a teacher. b) She doesn't have any regrets. c) Sometimes she wishes she had become an athlete.

b Listen again and find the answers to the questions.

4 Where did she go to college? How long was her journey?
5 Why couldn't she continue her gymnastics' training after she started college?
6 Where did she do her training 50 years ago? Where do athletes train today?

3 Down the rabbit hole

a *Alice's Adventures in Wonderland* is a story for children about a girl who finds herself in a place where she has many strange adventures. Read the three extracts and choose the best line to complete each extract.

1 'I wish I hadn't mentioned Dinah,' she said to herself.
2 'I do wish I hadn't drunk quite so much!'
3 'I wish I hadn't cried so much.'

b Why does Alice regret a) drinking from the bottle b) crying and c) talking about her cat?

c In groups, discuss the following.

- When you were a child, did you ever want to be bigger or smaller or different?
- Have you ever wished for something and then regretted that your wish came true?

Alice was just going to leave the room when she saw a little bottle ... 'I know something interesting is sure to happen,' she said to herself, 'whenever I eat or drink anything; so I'll just see what this does. I do hope it'll make me grow large again!' It did so indeed; before she had drunk half the bottle, she found her head pressing against the ceiling, and had to stoop to stop her neck from being broken. She put down the bottle, saying, 'That's quite enough - I hope I won't grow any more - as it is, I can't get out of the door.'

'... and things are worse than ever,' thought Alice, 'for I was never so small as this before, never!' And as she said this, her foot slipped, and splash! she was up to her chin in salt water. She soon realised that she was in the pool of tears which she had wept when she was nine feet high.

'Please come back and finish your story!' Alice called, but the mouse only walked a little quicker. 'I wish I had our Dinah here!' said Alice. 'She'd soon fetch it back!' 'And who is Dinah, if I might ask?' said one of the birds. Alice replied eagerly: 'Dinah's our cat, and she's such a capital one for catching mice. And, oh, you should see her after the birds! Why, she'll eat a little bird as soon as look at it!' This speech caused quite a sensation. Some of the birds hurried off at once and Alice was soon left alone.

4 Wordspot
vocabulary in context

a What are the people doing? Match the words to the pictures.

squatting kneeling slouching skipping diving stooping

b Now complete the sentences with a form of the words above. You will not need to use all the words.

1 He ___ into the clear water and swam to the far end of the pool.
2 The doorway was so low he had to ___ to avoid hitting his head.
3 There were no chairs, so the men had to ___ down to eat their lunch.
4 Stand up straight! Stop ___ !

5 Language focus
I wish I'd

a Look at this example:

I *wish* I hadn't drunk so much!

You use *wish* + past perfect to talk about regrets about the past.

b Use the prompts to write about things you wish you had/ hadn't done.

Example no umbrella/it's raining
   I wish I'd brought an umbrella.
1 no petrol/car has stopped
2 phone rang/dinner burned while you were speaking
3 didn't study/failed exams

was/were going to

a Look at this example:

You *were going to* be a gymnastics teacher, weren't you?

What was Helen intending to do? Did she do it?

b You use *was going to* to talk about things you intended to do in the past; usually they are things that you didn't do.

c Tell your partner about things you were *going to do/be/become*, but didn't. Give your reasons for not doing these things.

Example I was going to study art, but I changed my mind.

6 The Silent Couple

a In pairs, discuss the correct order for the events of the story, then listen and check your answers. (The ending is not given.)

1 The wife asked the husband to close the door and he refused.
2 The couple agreed that the first one to speak would close the door.
3 A husband and wife were relaxing in their new home after their wedding.
4 A policeman came, but the husband and wife wouldn't answer his questions.
5 The wife begged him not to hurt her husband.
6 The husband said the wife should close the door, and she refused.
7 Thieves robbed the husband and wife of everything.
8 The police officer threatened to hit the husband.

b In pairs, discuss how you think the story ends. What does the husband do next? Then listen to the end of the story. Were you correct?

7 Story-telling

Student A: think of a well-known story from your country and make notes. Tell the story to your partner, but let him/her guess the ending.

Student B: listen to your partner tell you a story. He/She will not tell you how the story ends. Tell your partner how you think the story ends.

UNIT 16

The weather

1 Saying what you think

a Where would you expect to find types of housing like those in the photographs? In what way(s) is/are each of them suitable for the weather/climate of the area you would find them in?

b Read the statements. For each one, say whether you think it is true, false or you don't know. Then discuss your opinions with a partner.

1 In hot Middle Eastern countries, people wear long, loose robes that are specially folded so that cold air is trapped inside.
2 People who live in colder climates can put on weight and become very depressed during the winter because there is less daylight.
3 In Southern Germany the accident, crime and suicide rates increase at the time of the Fohn winds.
4 Indians living in mountain villages at heights of 5,200 m (17,000 ft) have larger lungs and hearts so that they can breathe the thinner air.

c Make notes on how the weather affects your country. Think about:

housing   lifestyle   clothing   the people

Then discuss in groups.

2 Wordspot
word set

a Make a chart with the headings: *wind, wet weather, dry weather, temperature* and *seasons*, and put the following words under the correct heading.

spring   arid   showers   winter   humid   autumn   gusty
breezy   drought   freezing   storm   hurricane   warm
summer   monsoon   hot   flood

b Now write a paragraph describing the climate and seasons in your country.

3 Global warming

a Some scientists say that the earth is getting warmer. Do you agree with them? If so, do you think it is a serious problem? Why?/Why not?

b Listen to a radio discussion with a climate expert who has been studying global warming and answer the questions.

1 Dr Stokes says that the carbon dioxide in the atmosphere is 'like a blanket around the earth' Explain what she means by this.
2 If the earth's temperature rose by 2°C (4°F), what would happen to the polar ice caps and coastal cities?
3 Complete these warnings:

a Unless we act now, more and more __ because their croplands have become deserts.
b Even if we start to make changes now, we __ reverse all the damage.
c But unless we can reduce the amount of carbon dioxide going into the atmosphere, we're going to have __.

4 The greenhouse effect

a The generally accepted theory is that global warming is caused by the greenhouse effect. Study the flowchart and match each of the texts with the appropriate part of the flowchart.

b Study the flowchart and make notes about a) the causes and b) the effects of global warming. In pairs, compare your notes.

a Burning oil puts CO2 into the atmosphere, and the number of cars in the world is increasing.

b CFC molecules from aerosol containers and refrigerators also contribute to global warming. One CFC molecule has the same greenhouse warming effect as 10,000 molecules of CO2.

c The carbon dioxide (CO2) in the atmosphere traps the heat when it is reflected back from the earth. The more CO2 there is in the atmosphere, the more heat is trapped. This causes global warming.

d About 6 billion tons of carbon dioxide from fossil fuels (coal, oil, peat) are being thrown into the atmosphere every year.

e A lot of carbon dioxide comes from burning forests, and more than 26 million acres of forest are being destroyed every year.

f All this creates climatic problems. Floods: sea levels have risen. Droughts: the US droughts of 1988 could become commonplace.

g Solar heat is radiated to the earth. It passes through the atmosphere and warms the land and sea.

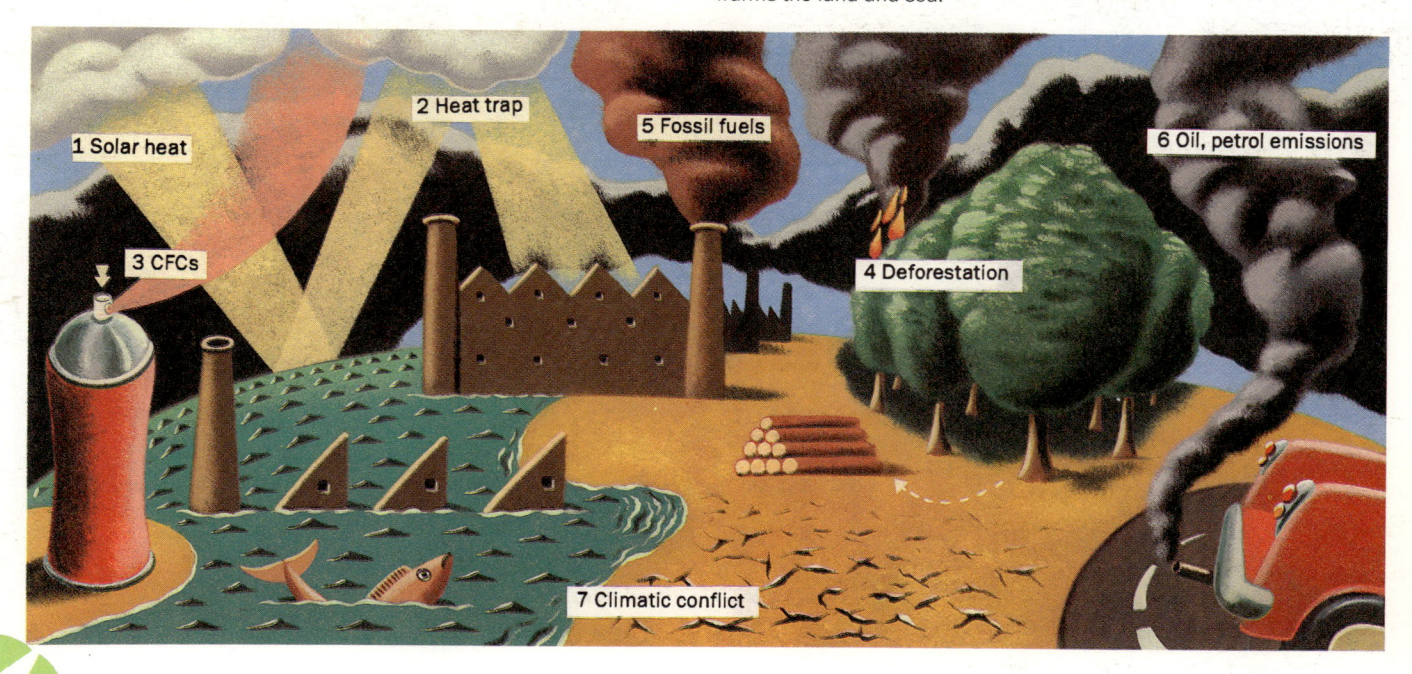

1 Solar heat
2 Heat trap
3 CFCs
4 Deforestation
5 Fossil fuels
6 Oil, petrol emissions
7 Climatic conflict

5 Language focus
unless

a Look at the example:

Unless we act now, more and more people will starve.

Unless has the meaning of *if .. not*. It is often used in warnings.

Example If we don't act now, more and more people will starve.

b Use the prompts to write warnings about global warming.

Example slow down/global warming/we/have more droughts

Unless we slow down global warming, we will have more droughts.

1 burn fewer trees/global warming/continue
2 reduce the CO2 going into the atmosphere/polar ice caps/melt
3 slow down global warming/many more people/starve
4 act now/we/have serious problems in the future

c Write two more warnings of your own.

6 Discussion

a In groups, agree on practical solutions to the problem of global warming.

Example I think governments should make cars illegal. That's a good idea./I disagree. I think they should put a high tax on petrol and use the money to develop electric/solar cars.

b When you have finished, read your list of solutions to the class. As a class, decide which group made the best suggestions.

7 Sayings

a What do you think these well-known expressions mean? Discuss in pairs.

1 It's raining cats and dogs.
2 I'm saving for a rainy day.

Do you have any similar expressions in your own language?

b In pairs, prepare an advertisement to warn people about the dangers of global warming.

UNIT 17 You and your health

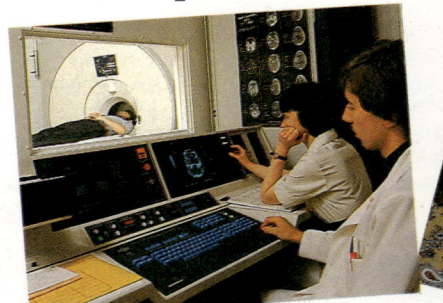

1 Saying what you think

a Which of these types of treatment do you associate with a) conventional western medicine b) alternative medicine?

acupuncture   antibiotics   aromatherapy   drugs   homeopathy   natural remedies
surgery   tablets   vaccinations   X-rays

b Have you or has anyone you know ever used any of the alternative forms of healing above? Are there any that you would or would not use? Give reasons.

Homeopathy involves using tiny amounts of natural substances which are said to activate the body's own 'healing force'. At a first consultation, a homeopathic practitioner will try to build up a complete picture of a patient, and to do this will ask a wide-ranging series of questions.

At the age of 28, Ian Brice was a physical wreck. His feet were badly deformed, his joints ached and his knees had swollen. His doctor told him he had rheumatoid arthritis - and that there was no cure for it. For eight years Ian used drugs and pain-killers, but these brought problems of their own.

'The side effects were just terrible,' said Ian, 'I was sick and came out in rashes.' Eventually a friend suggested homeopathy. 'The doctor asked me everything, what I ate, what I liked and didn't like, even what I wore in bed,' said Ian. 'Then he said he thought he could cure me.'

Within a month of taking the American tea, Ledum or Marsh tea, the difference was dramatic. 'My aches and pains just went away,' said Ian. Five months later he was playing tennis. Now a year later, he plays football with his son.

Jan Smith decided to visit her doctor when her leg suddenly became very red and swollen. Her doctor diagnosed a blood clot, and told her that it could easily be cured with drugs and regular visits to hospital. Ignoring her doctor's advice, she decided to treat the condition herself with herbal remedies which she bought from a local health food shop. The clot moved quickly through her body to her lungs, and within days of seeing her doctor, Ms Smith was dead.

2 The choice is yours

a Read about the experiences of two people and answer the questions.

1 Why do you think Ian Brice found it difficult to walk?
2 What happened when he tried conventional medicines?
3 Why do you think the homeopathic doctor asked him so many questions?
4 What were Jan's symptoms?
5 Why do you think she ignored the doctor's advice?

b Now close your book and retell one of the stories.

3 Doctor's orders

a Listen to this conversation between a doctor and her patient, and answer the questions.

1 What are Mr Duncan's symptoms?
2 What does the doctor diagnose?
3 What treatment does the patient need?

b Listen again. Which of these sentences does the doctor actually say?

1. What's the problem? 2. Can you describe the pain? 3. Just sit down here. 4. How long have you had this pain? 5. Are you drinking much? 6. Do you feel feverish? 7. Take off your shirt. 8. Show me where it hurts the most. 9. Tell me if it hurts. 10. Lie here while I call the nurse.

c Listen again and correct the sentences that she did not say.

33

4 Wordspot
word set

a Which of the following words and phrases are a) a symptom or an injury b) an illness or c) a type of treatment?

aching/swollen joints   rheumatoid arthritis   pain-killers   rash   blood clot   herbal remedy   appendicitis   fever   sore throat   tonsillitis   antibiotics   migraine   nausea   headache

b What other words do you know for each of these categories?

c Find out how people treat the following in your partner's country.

influenza   headache   minor burns   nose bleed

5 Language focus
indirect questions

a Look at two of the questions the homeopath asked Ian:

1 Do you eat meat?
2 What do you wear in bed?

If these questions were indirect, they would read:

1 The doctor asked Ian if he ate meat.
2 The doctor asked Ian what he wore in bed.

How do indirect questions differ from direct questions in word order, punctuation and tense?

b When you report a yes/no question, you use a clause beginning with *if* (1); when you report a question beginning with a question word (*what, who*), you use a clause beginning with the question word (2).

c Now write the doctor's questions in exercise 3 as indirect questions.

Example The doctor asked the patient what the problem was.

indirect orders

a Look at this example:

The doctor told Mr Duncan to lie down.

b If someone orders or tells someone to do something, you can report this using *tell* + to-infinitive.

c Write the doctor's orders and advice in exercise 3 as indirect speech.

Example The doctor told Mr Duncan to pull up his shirt.

6 Roleplay

a Listen to two conversations in a doctor's surgery and complete a doctor's report for each conversation, using these headings:

Symptoms   Length of illness   Frequency of illness   Diagnosis   Treatment

b *Student A*: Ask Student B about his/her visit to the doctor.
Student B: You are one of the patients on the tape. Tell Student A what the doctor asked you, what he diagnosed and what treatment he recommended.

7 Tried and tested

Read these herbal remedies and match them with the common complaint they can be used to cure.

1 Drink a hot infusion of chamomile flowers, fennel or sage leaves.
2 Rub an ointment made of thyme and summer savory onto the skin. For quick relief, squeeze parsley juice on to the affected area.
3 Drink an infusion of lemon balm, and apply a few drops of either oil of marjoram or oil of peppermint to the place where it hurts.

a) insect bites/stings   b) toothache   c) a cold

UNIT 18

Mysteries

1 Saying what you think

1 The American handed Leamas another cup of coffee and said, 'Why don't you go and get some sleep. We can ring you if he shows up.'

2 Once, when Benet was about fourteen, they had been in a train together, alone in the carriage, and Mopsa had tried to stab her with a carving knife.

3 The thin air of Mars was chill but not really cold.

4 For two days they had seen no other traveller, not even a solitary cowhand or an Indian.

a Match the opening lines to the books. Which of these categories do the books belong to: murder, mystery, a spy novel, western, science fiction? What other categories can you think of to describe types of books?

b Which of these books do you think you would like to read? Why?

Donald Mallinson

Celia Mallinson

Laura Pagett

Tessa Mallinson

Detective Chief Inspector Finch

2 Whodunnit?

It is Christmas Eve and Detective Chief Inspector Finch has checked into a hotel. As he is standing in reception a party of people check in.

a Read Inspector Finch's account of the story so far. Who could have killed Celia Mallinson, and why? Read the story again. Then in pairs, make a list of five suspects. Beside their names write their motive, or reason for murdering her.

b Now listen to Inspector Finch's list of suspects and their motives. Were there any differences between his list and yours? Tell the class.

A cold and frosty morning
I thought at first that Celia Mallinson was dark-haired, like her friend, Laura Pagett, but when she took off her fur hat I realised that she was blonde. The Mallinson's, I thought, were not a happy family - Donald Mallinson was obviously bored with his wife, and their daughter, Tessa, appeared to hate her mother. Laura seemed pleasant, and I learned that her husband was expected to arrive later. Later, I overheard an angry conversation between Celia Mallinson and a man called Lawrence Dean. Dean, I discovered, was a former lover whom Mrs Mallinson had rejected. He strode off angrily, and I followed Mrs Mallinson into the hotel bar.

There she saw her daughter, Tessa, flirting with the barman. I heard Mrs Mallinson threaten to have the barman fired if he didn't leave Tessa alone. This embarrassed Tessa and made the barman very angry.

After dinner, I saw Celia Mallinson again. This time she was standing by the door in her fur coat and hat. Celia was on her way outside to look for Tessa, who she believed was with the barman. When Laura Pagett tried to stop her, Celia threatened to tell Laura's husband that Laura was planning to divorce him and take her money out of his business. 'I told you that in confidence,' whispered Laura as Celia stormed out.

I went up to my room, but shortly after midnight I was woken and told that Celia Mallinson had been murdered. Downstairs were the shocked Mallinson family, the hotel manager, and Mr Pagett, who said that he had arrived ten minutes before from London. As I was leaving the hotel to view the body, I saw the hotel manager trying to move Mr Pagett's car from the front of the hotel. I noticed that the car was slow to start and that it was emitting heavy fumes from the exhaust. They took me to view Celia Mallinson's body - her killer had hit her on the back of the head and thrown her over a bridge.

3 The solution

a In pairs, decide who killed Celia Mallinson using your list of suspects from exercise 2. Give your reasons and tell the class.

b Now listen to Inspector Finch tell the end of the story. Were you correct?

c Listen again and find answers to these questions:
1 What did Pagett think when he saw Celia? Why?
2 When did Pagett arrive from London?
3 How did Inspector Finch know when Pagett had arrived?
4 What did Pagett do when he realised his mistake?

4 Language focus
could have done

a Look at this example:

Laura Pagett *could/may/might/ have killed* Celia Mallinson.

Is the speaker saying that a) Laura was definitely the killer or b) it is possible that Laura was the killer? How do you know?

b Now say what could have happened in these situations:

Example A burglar has been in your house. You think you forgot to lock a window. - He could have got in through the window.

1 You arrive home and discover that the meat you left out for dinner has gone. You left a window open and your neighbours have a cat.
2 You receive a very high telephone bill. A friend stayed at your house for a week while you were on holiday.
3 You arrive at work/school and discover that you don't have your purse/wallet with you.
4 You arrive home and discover that your house is on fire.

5 Wordspot
phrasal verbs

a Look at the dictionary entry. What is the meaning of *get away with* in the sentence below?

If Finch hadn't seen the manager trying to start his car, Pagett might have got away with murdering Celia Mallinson.

> **get away with.** If you get away with something, you are not punished for doing something the you should not do. EG Nobody gets away with tearing my coat ... He might have bribed her - and got away with it. to get away with murder: see murder.

b Complete the sentences with a form of these phrasal verbs.

get down to   get on to   get over with   get round to

1 It's getting late. It's time I __ work. (*started*)
2 I never seem to __ doing my homework. (*find the time to*)
3 Can you hurry? I'd like to __ this job __ .(*finish*)
4 Let's not __ politics or religion again - we'll only argue. (*start discussing*)

6 Discussion

a In groups, think of as many possible explanations for these situations as you can.

1 The police break into a locked flat. They find John and Mary dead on the floor. They are naked and lying in a pool of water.
The window is open and there is broken glass on the floor. How did John and Mary die?
2 On a very hot day, a man is found in the middle of a completely empty room. He has hanged himself. There is a van outside and a puddle of water on the floor. How did the man manage to hang himself in an empty room?

b When you have finished, read your ideas to the class. The class should vote on which group came up with the best ideas.

7 Survey

Read the questions, and write two more of your own. Then ask your partner.

1 What is your favourite type of book?
2 What is the last book that you read? Did you enjoy it?
3 Have you ever read a book by Agatha Christie?
4 Who is your favourite author?

UNIT 19

Places in time

a
b
c
d

Rio de Janeiro
Location: Brazil, coastal city
Climate: hot and humid all year round
Special features/attractions: carnival; statue of Christ on Corcovado Mountain; Copacabana beach

Hong Kong
Location: South China Sea
Climate: hot summers; rainy season from June to August; cold winters
Special features/attractions: shopping; Aberdeen Harbour; Victoria Peak

Istanbul
Location: Turkey, on the Bosphorus
Climate: very hot, humid summers; cold winters, some snow
Special features/attractions: excellent views; Blue Mosque

Venice
Location: Italy
Climate: hot summers; cold winters
Special features/attractions: canals; Doge's Palace; St Mark's Square views

1 Saying what you think

a Match the photographs of the cities with the notes.

b Which of these cities would you prefer to visit/live in? Which would you least like to visit/live in? Give reasons for your choices.

1 Surrounded by hills and vast deserts, lies a poor, Syrian oasis town. In this town, freshly picked dates lie heaped along the main street. There are no carpets or luxuries for sale. The local restaurant is a bare cafe with neon lights and a juke box. Yet, 2,000 years ago, this forgotten oasis town was the fabulous classical city of Palmyra.
2 The rise of Palmyra began nearly 3,000 years ago. A key staging post on the famous Silk Route from China and the east to the Mediterranean, Palmyra provided essential services to the traders.
3 Palmyra became a city full of eastern riches - jade and priceless silk from China, perfumes, spices and jewels, carpets and glassware. By 200 AD the population of Palmyra had reached nearly a quarter of a million. It had theatres, libraries, banks, temples and a Senate House.
4 But by the sixth century the desert trading routes began to decline and so did Palmyra. A few hundred years later the city was finally destroyed by a severe earthquake.
5 In the last fifty years, Palmyra has been excavated and some of its buildings have been restored. The site now covers an area of 6 square kilometres - and only one quarter of the original city has been discovered so far.
6 Palmyra is one of the ancient wonders of the world, but already the new merchants are moving in - a new international hotel and airstrip have just been built there to attract tourists. Will Palmyra rise again - as a city of international hotel blocks, swimming pools and tourist shops?

2 Travellers' tales

a Listen to these people who have lived in or visited the cities in exercise 1. Which city is each speaker talking about? How do you know?

b Listen again. For each city make notes about a) what the speaker likes about the city b) the city's problems and/or what the speaker doesn't like about the city. Compare your notes with a partner.

3 Sands of time

a Make a list of ancient cities that you know of. Which of the cities on your list are still important cities, and which are not?

b Read the text about the ancient city of Palmyra and find the answers to these questions:

1 Why did Palmyra become important 3,000 years ago?
2 Is it still an important city? Why?/Why not?
3 What has been done to Palmyra in the last fifty years?
4 What could happen to Palmyra in the future?

c These are the topics of the six paragraphs of the text. Read the text again and match each paragraph to a topic.

The destruction of Palmyra.   The possible future of Palmyra.
Description of Palmyra today.   The excavation of Palmyra.
Description of Palmyra 2,000 years ago.   Why Palmyra became wealthy.

4 Wordspot
participles as adjectives

a Look at these examples:

1 ... *freshly* picked dates
2 ... this *forgotten* oasis town

A large number of English adjectives *(picked, forgotten)* have the same form as the past participle of a verb. An adverb of manner *(freshly)* or degree *(well)* is often used in front of these adjectives.

b Use an adverb from A and a participle as adjective from B to complete each of the sentences.

A: badly   freshly   well
B: bake   break   know   paint   pay

Example He doesn't like his job, but he keeps it because it's well-paid.

1 I'm surprised you haven't heard of Ted. He's quite a __ actor.
2 Mhmm! I love the smell of __ bread.
3 Careful! Don't touch the walls! They're all __.
4 He'll be on crutches for months. His leg is very __.

5 Language focus
has been done

a Look at these examples:

1 In the last fifty years, Palmyra *has been excavated* ...
2 ... and some of its buildings *have been restored*.

What tense are the verbs in? Are the sentences in the active or passive? Why?

b Imagine you are in Palmyra in five years time. Write sentences about what has been done.

Example many more houses/construct
Many more houses have been constructed.

1 trees/plant   2 the entire city/excavate
3 museum/build   4 the local restaurant/tear down

c What has been done in your town in the last five years?

6 Discussion

Student A: Ask Student B about the city he/she lives in or has visited. Ask about: location, weather, interesting things to do, the food, what he/she likes/liked or doesn't/didn't like about the city.

Example Where is it (located)? What's the weather like?

Student B: Answer Student A's questions.

Example It's in the north of .../near the sea
... In the summer it's ... but in the winter ...

7 City sights

a What do you think this well-known expression means?

When in Rome, do as the Romans do.

Can you say the expression in your own words?

b Look at the photographs of well-known cities at the turn of the century. How many of them can you recognise?

UNIT 20 Leaders

1 Saying what you think

a Which of these qualities do you think are important for a leader to have?

ambition charisma confidence decisiveness efficiency energy intelligence talent other

b In pairs, compare your answers. Would you add any qualities to the list? Agree on five qualities.

c Can you think of a leader who has/had any or all of these qualities? Who is/was he/she?

2 Born or made?

a This is a discussion with a psychotherapist about leadership. Listen to Part 1 of the discussion, and note down the personal qualities she says a leader should have.

b Now listen to the second part of the discussion.

1 What personal quality does the psychotherapist say a leader is born with?
2 In what two ways can leadership abilities be developed?

c The psychotherapist talks about authoritarian and democratic styles of leadership. Read the definitions and then decide which leadership styles you think the phrases refer to.

Something that is *democratic* is based on the idea that everyone should have equal rights and should be involved in making important decisions.

Someone who is *authoritarian* wants to control other people rather than letting them decide things for themselves.

- Firm, definite, unbending.
- Likes to include all the group members in the decision making.
- Sometimes the group members are not sure who is in charge.
- May not want to take advice.

d Now listen to Part 3 of the tape and check your answers to part c. Which leadership style does she think is best? Why?

3 Quiz

a Are you a follower or a leader? Give yourself marks on a scale of 1 to 10 for your leadership abilities. (1 is a follower and 10 is a leader.)

b Now do the quiz and look up the scores and results on page 60 How did the quiz results compare with your own assessment in part a?

c Compare your results in groups. Do you agree with the results of the quiz? Why?/Why not?

---

1 You're sitting with some colleagues at work and someone says they'd like a cup of coffee. Do you:
a Offer to make everyone a cup.
b Say you'd like one too.
c Ask the most junior person to make it.
d Tell the person to get him/herself one then.

2 Your best friend gets promoted at work. How would you react?
a You'd be very pleased for him/her.
b You'd ask him/her for advice.
c You'd act pleased but be jealous inside.
d You'd congratulate him/her for finally catching up with you!

3 You get reprimanded at work or get a bad mark at school. How do you feel?
a Terrible.
b Upset, but you understand why.
c You don't let it bother you too much.
d You refuse to accept it and go to see your boss/teacher about it.

4 As regards socialising, do your friends:
a Make the arrangements and phone you with the plan.
b All decide together.
c Phone you for the plan.
d It varies.

5 At school, how is/was your general behaviour?
a Excellent. You worked hard.
b You appeared to be good, but you were often misbehaving secretly.
c You were openly loud and badly behaved.
d Terrible.

6 A friend/colleague shares a huge secret with you. How tempted are you to tell?
a You're not tempted.
b You have to tell your spouse/best friend.
c You tell everyone about a month later.
d You tell everyone.

4 Language focus
articles: *a an the*

a You can use the indefinite article *a* or *an*
   a) when you mention someone or something for the first time
   b) after *to be* to describe someone's qualities:
   You *are an extrovert*.

b You can use *the* with a noun if it is obvious who or what you are referring to
   a) from what has already been said/written
   b) because there is a prepositional phrase after the noun:
   You can often see *the way to solve problems*.
   c) because there is an adjective in front of the noun:
   You follow *the right people*.

c Why is an article not necessary in front of the nouns in these sentences?

   You're not worried about *people* liking you.
   Leaders don't always follow the rules.

d Complete the texts with *a*, *an*, or *the*. One of the sentences does not require an article. Why not?
   1 You're __ shy, quiet person, who probably has just a few, close friends.
   2 Don't let __ people order you around.
   3 You're too selfish to think seriously about __ needs of other people.
   4 You're __ follower, not __ leader.
   5 Assert yourself in __ right areas, and you will succeed.

5 Wordspot
describing character

a Write the words and phrases under the correct heading - *a* or *an*.

   ambitious man   born leader   European language   L-shaped room   hand
   honest politician   language   T-shirt   union leader

b Why did you use *a* or *an* in the examples above?

6 Discussion

a What groups do you belong to? Make a list. Think about:
   family   friends   study   work   religion   nationality   other

b Work in groups. Say which of the groups in part a is most/least important to you and why.

7 Phrases

a Use some of the words below to complete the sentences.
   demonstration   life   singer   took   way   give   a group
   1 Follow me. I'll lead the __ to your room.
   2 You've been everywhere. You certainly have led an exciting __.
   3 He's the lead __ in a rock group.
   4 France __ the lead in the development of the airbus.
   5 The political __ was led by a group of angry students.

b Think of a leader or well-known person. Write down three facts about him/her, but don't write his/her name. Can the class guess who you are writing about?

UNIT 1 PRACTICE SECTION

1 For each of the objects below, write a sentence saying what you use it for, using *to* + infinitive.

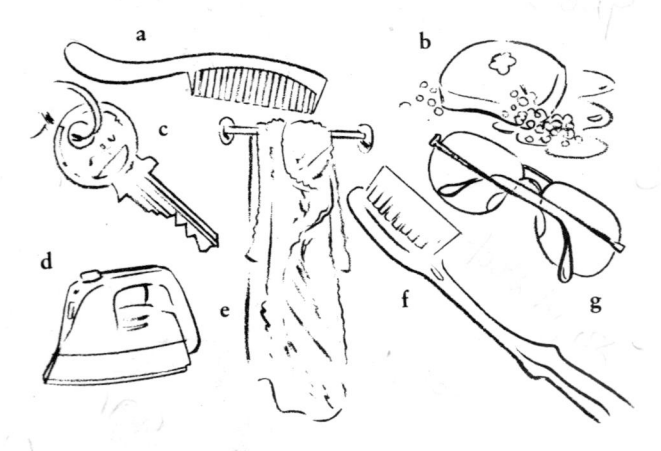

Example a - I use a comb to comb/tidy my hair.

b..
c..
d..
e..
f..
g..

2 Now write about five gestures and what they mean to you. Use *to* + infinitive.

Example I cross my fingers to mean/indicate 'good luck'.

3 Look at the pictures. Choose the word below that you think best describes the way that each person is feeling.

frustrated   afraid   angry   surprised   confident   happy

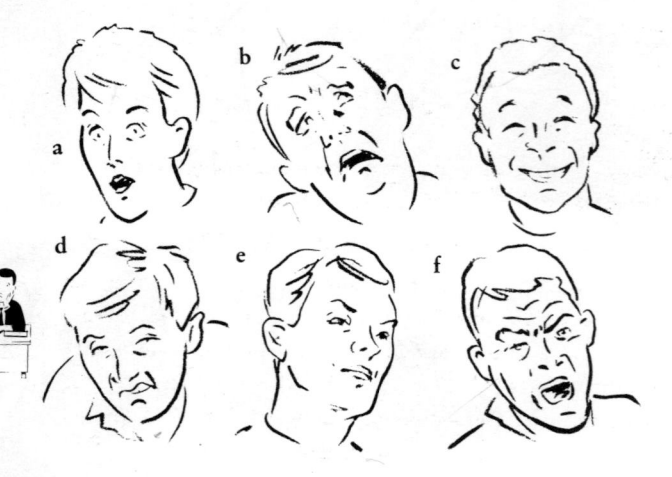

a..
b..
c..
d..
e..
f..

What other words could you use to describe their feelings?

4 Complete each sentence with the *-ing* or *-ed* form of one of the words below.

disappoint   fright   annoy   embarrass   excite

1 Your exam results were .... - I was sure they'd be better.
2 I'm so .... about my holiday - I can hardly wait!
3 Please don't be .... with me - I didn't mean to crash the car.
4 Don't be .... Anyone can make a fool of themselves.
5 I was .... in the play - it wasn't as funny as I expected.
6 Come and enjoy an .... day out in London!
7 'Don't be scared.' 'I am. I'm .... of the dark.'

5 Complete the definitions, using words from the unit.

1 A g..st..r.. is a movement made to express information or emotion.
2 Your p..st..r.. is the way you sit or stand.
3 Your f..c..l expression is the look on your face.
4 N..n-v..rb..l communication is communication without words.
5 If you lack s..lf-c..nf..d..nc.., then you are not sure of your own abilities.

6 Revision

Read this extract from a newspaper article on body language and fill in the spaces using the following verbs:

are   are   deals   have   have to   help   is   revolves
says   says   touch   use   work

'Background and profession [1]......... key influences to how well we [2]......... body language,' [3]......... body language expert Gordon Wainwright. People in the world of show business [4].......... famous for shouting 'dahling!' and kissing all and sundry, while people who [5].......... in London do not [6].......... any more than they can [7]......... - a brief handshake [8].......... their limit. Mr Wainwright [9].........: 'Entertainers [10].......... interact with their audience, and anyone who [11].......... with people - doctors, nurses, teachers, shop assistants, will [12].......... better body language than someone whose work [13].........

UNIT 2

PRACTICE SECTION

1 Use gerunds to finish these sentences.

Example I like
I like studying English.

1 I don't enjoy..... *gardening* ....
2 I hate/can't stand... *getting on the bus*..
3 .... *Working* ...... takes up most of my day.
4 ..... *Swimming* ... is a sport/pastime that I really enjoy.

2 Look back at exercise 5 (page 4) and write the opposites of these words in the sentences below.

attractive   correct   educated   legal   patient   popular   safe

1 'Can't you hurry? We're going to be late!' 'Don't be so ....'
2 He's never been to school. In fact, he's totally ....
3 He was arrested by the police for .... activities.
4 It's horrible! It's the most .... piece of furniture I've ever seen!
5 The answer you gave me was ....
6 When they investigated the accident they found that conditions in the factory were ....
7 The Government was defeated after a series of .... decisions.

3 Complete each sentence using a form of the word in brackets.

Example They have always had a happy *marriage* (*marry*)

1 It's important for children to have a good .... (*educate*)
2 Children in poor countries can be helped by .... (*sponsor*)
3 The man they arrested already had two .... for theft. (*convict*)
4 Ademma goes to a .... school and to a state school. (*supplement*)
5 It's a huge .... project. (*develop*)

4 Revision

Write what you are allowed or forbidden to do in the following pictures. Use *can* or *can't* in your answers.

Example a You can park here

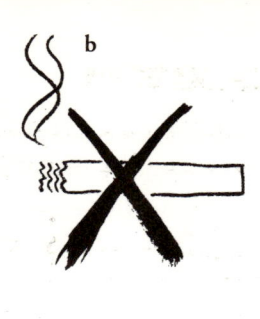

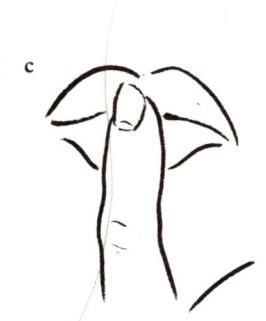

b ....
c ....
d ....
e ....
f ....

5 Complete the text using either the gerund (*-ing*) or the infinitive (*to* + verb) of the words below:

be   become   read   study   write   write

When I was a child, I always wanted [1]..*to be*.... either a teacher or a writer. English was my best subject: I liked [2]..*writing*.. and I loved [3]..*reading*.. essays. Eventually, I went to university [4]..*to study*.. English, and [5]..*becoming*.. . a teacher. I've never regretted it, but I still think I would like [6]..*to write*..... some day.

(42)

UNIT 3 PRACTICE SECTION

1
Rewrite each sentence to include the information in brackets. Use a non-defining relative clause.

Example Cats can see in the dark. (*hunt at night*)
Cats, who hunt at night, can see in the dark.

1 Gonzales is here to study English. (*arrived about three months ago*) *Gonzales, who arrived about three months ago, is here to study English.*

2 Alice teaches at a college. (*graduated last year*) *Alice, who graduated last year, teaches at a college.*

3 Some animals have large ears. (*help them to hear*) *Some animals have large ears, which helps them to hear.*

4 My father lives in Canada. (*retired five years ago*) *My father, who retired five years ago, lives in Canada.*

5 Fish 'hear' by feeling vibrations in the water. (*don't have ears*) *Fish, which does not have ears, 'hear' by feeling vibrations in the water.*

2
Join each of the sets of sentences. Do not use *it* or *them*.

Example Sweets are bad for you. I like *them* very much.
Sweets, which I like very much, are bad for you.

1 I lent him my favourite jacket. He lost *it*. ....

2 Heavy metal music is not as popular as it used to be. I hate *it*. ....

3 He's wearing a red, silk tie. I gave *it* to him for his birthday. ....

4 French perfume can be very expensive. I wear *it* on special occasions. ....

5 Snakes are my favourite animals. Some people keep *them* as pets. ....

Now complete these sentences. Use a non-defining relative clause.

6 London, ..., is the capital city of Britain.
7 My teacher, ..., seems to work very hard.
8 My parents, ..., did a wonderful job raising me.

3
Complete the tables with other forms of the words:

Noun	Verb	Verb	Noun
survival	....	interpret	....
stimulus	....	form	....
information	....	adapt	....

4
Use these words to complete the text.

a blind French idea pupil read soldiers they to used

Nowadays, Braille, the famous reading system for the blind, is [1] *used* worldwide. But until the 19th century, lettering for the [2] *blind* was simply raised alphabet letters. Then in 1819, a [3] *soldiers* captain invented a system that soldiers could use to [4] *read* at night. Captain Charles Barbier de la Serre invented [5] *a* system of raised dots and dashes on cardboard that [6] *they* could read with their fingertips. Barbier took his idea [7] *to* the Institute for the Young Blind in Paris, but [8] *French* said it was too complicated. But a young blind [9] *pupil* at the Institute, Louis Braille, decided to simplify the [10] *idea*, and the rest is history.

5
Complete each sentence with a form of one of the phrasal verbs below.

listen in   touch down   touch on   watch out
watch over

1 Be careful what you say - if you *touch on* a sensitive subject, you'll upset him.
2 It's not polite to *listen in* on a private conversation.
3 The mothers took turns *watch over* the children.
4 He watched the plane as it *touch down* on the runway.
5 If you don't *watch out*, you'll hurt yourself.

6 Revision

Decide whether the words in italics give extra information about the noun. If they do, write in the commas around them.

1 Animals *which hunt at night* often have big eyes.
2 Andrew *who is a banker* travels to London daily.
3 Flies *which taste with their feet* walk over their food before they eat it.
4 People *who are blind* often have a strong sense of touch.
5 The skin *which is the organ for sensing touch* is covered with sensitive nerve endings.

UNIT 4

PRACTICE SECTION

1 Read the newspaper extracts and complete the sentences. Write the verbs in brackets in the past simple or present perfect.

1 The Prince and Princess [1]........... (*begin*) their tour of Thailand. They [2]........... (*arrive*) in Bangkok this morning.

2 Another cat [3]........... (*die*) from a mystery disease. A scientist [4]........... (*warn*) yesterday that thousands of pets could already have the disease.

3 A couple [5]........... (*win*) their fight for permission to split their home in two. Michael and Jill Webb, [6]........... (*live*) separately in their luxury farmhouse for three years. Six months ago, they [7]........... (*apply*) to the local council to build a dividing wall. At first, the council [8]........... (*refuse*) them permission, but the Environment Department ...

2 Use the verbs below in the correct tense to complete the article.

be   confiscate   face   find   get   open   plan

A Swedish customs official [1]........... a suitcase full of snakes. The customs man [2]........... the case during a routine customs check, and [3]........... 37 snakes, including a python. The suitcase owner, a Dane who now [4]........... a smuggling charge, said he [5]........... to sell the snakes, nine of which [6]........... poisonous. A customs official said: 'We [7]........... used to these sort of things.'

3 Match the headlines with the news reports.

a **Drug crimes**   b **Bomb scare**   c **Voted out!**

d **Express record**   e **Power overload**

1 Two bombs were defused in London today, after a man called to tell police where the bombs were ...

2 The Government resigned last night after a vote of no-confidence ...

3 People ran for cover when their TV sets and microwaves suddenly blew up yesterday. A freak surge in the electricity supply ...

4 The French high-speed TGV train broke its own speed record for the second time ...

5 Police fear drug-taking will be the most serious crime in Britain by the year 2000 ...

4 The article in exercise 2 (page 7) says:

Only time will tell whether they head out or *come back* in again.

Look at part of the dictionary entry for the phrasal verb *come back*. Which meaning of the phrasal verb is nearest in meaning to the one in the example above?

Come back. 1 To **come back** somewhere means to return to that place. 2 To **come back** to a topic, question, idea means to return to it ... 3 If a scene, event, name, etc that you had forgotten **comes back** to you, you remember it ...

Complete the sentences with *come* in the correct form + *back, between, by, into* or *off*.

1 I don't want to .... you and your parents.
2 He's out of work and finding a job very hard to ....
3 She .... some money after her uncle's death.
4 He tugged at the handle and it .... in his hand.
5 I'll .... to that question later on.

5 Which of the words below do you associate with newspapers, which with radio or television, and which with both? Write the words under the appropriate headings.

article   broadcast   a column   documentary   editor   headline   letter to the editor   journalist   newsreader   reporter   series   transmit/transmission

Newspaper	Radio/television	Both

6 Revision

A journalist interviewed one of the men who rescued the whales. These are the man's answers. Write the journalist's questions.

Example 40. How many whales were stranded?

1 Two...........
2 Exhaustion...........
3 Canada's Fisheries Department...........
4 £00...........
5 Freezing...........

UNIT 5

PRACTICE SECTION

1 For each sentence, choose the correct word from the words in brackets.

1 He's a very (*cautious/cautiously*) driver.
2 It was a (*pleasant/pleasantly*) afternoon.
3 He drives (*cautious/cautiously*) since his accident.
4 He wrapped the gift (*careful/carefully*).
5 He smiled at us (*pleasant/pleasantly*).
6 They are a very (*happy/happily*) couple.
7 I thought it was a (*terrible/terribly*) accident.
8 They were sitting (*happy/happily*) in the car.

2 Complete the sentences with the adverb form of one of the adjectives below.

careless   cheap   fluent   gentle   polite   quick   quiet

1 'Do you speak Japanese well?' 'Oh yes, I speak it ....'
2 He placed the glass .... on the edge of the table and it fell off and broke.
3 They finished the job .... so that they could leave work early.
4 It was a bargain - I got it very .... in a sale.
5 They spoke .... so as not to wake the children.
6 Although he was angry, he answered me ....
7 She wiped the tears .... from the child's face.

3 Complete these sentences with *good* or *well*.

1 He sings very ....
2 It tastes ....
3 You play the piano ....
4 Dinner smells ....
5 He drives ....
6 It looks ....
7 You write ....
8 That sounds ....
9 That feels ....

4 Use the words below to complete the text.

deeply   injury   finally   soon   immediately   on fire   put   lucky

My brother put out the flames

It was midnight on May 9 1987, when Neil Rodgers saw his 15-year-old sister Zoe rush out of the kitchen ¹............ Their parents were out at a party but due back at their Sheffield home ²............

Although only 12 at the time, Neil ripped off Zoe's top and quickly stamped out the flames. He then ³............ her under a cold shower, and ⁴............ telephoned his aunt, who took them both to hospital.
He's modest about his hero's role, but his mother, Betty, ⁵............ admires his courage and acknowledges the role he played in reducing the ⁶............ his sister suffered.
'Even though he won't admit it,' says Betty, 'he was crying when his father and I ⁷............ arrived at the hospital. Zoe still had to spend five weeks in hospital and have three skin grafts, but we're ⁸............ it wasn't worse.'

5 Complete the sentences using *by* + *-ing*.

1 Richard saved Zoe's life ....
2 He put out the flames ....
3 He cooled Zoe's burns ....
4 He got help ....

Now answer these questions using *by* + *-ing*.

5 How do people show that they are happy or pleased? ....
6 How do babies show that they have had enough milk? ....
7 How can you improve your reading speed? ....

6 Revision

Answer the questions about Janice and Richard using *to* + infinitive.

Example Why did Janice organise bandages, prepare makeshift beds and make coffee? - To help the other people on the ferry.

1 Why did her father 'act as a human bridge'? ....
2 Why did Richard rip off Zoe's top and stamp out the flames? ....
3 Why did he put Zoe under a cold shower? ....
4 Why did he ring his aunt? ....
5 Why did Zoe have to spend five weeks in hospital? ....

45

UNIT 6 PRACTICE SECTION

1 Complete these sentences about the Amish with *allowed to*, *supposed to* or *not allowed/supposed to*.

1 The Amish are very religious. They are .... pray daily.
2 The women have long hair. They are .... cut it.
3 The women wear mostly black, but they are .... wear brightly coloured blouses.
4 Most sports are discouraged, but they are .... swim.
5 They are .... live in the way that Joseph Ammann said that they should live.
6 They are .... make use of 20th century technology.

2 Finish these sentences about your life when you were a child.

1 When I was a child, I was supposed to ....
....
2 I was allowed to ....
....
3 I wasn't supposed/allowed to ....
....
4 I was forbidden to ....
....

3 Use the words and phrases below to complete the text.

as long as   because   however   the next day
so   soon   when

¹.......... she wanted a loan to turn her farmhouse into a hotel, Jane Stanbury got a frosty reception from local banks. They refused to lend her money ²............... . she had no experience and could provide no security for the money. ³................ Jane invited her bank manager around for a meal and after a taste of her cooking he ⁴............ changed his mind. As Jane says, 'He called me ⁵............... and said "Here's £10,000 - just ask if you need any more."' The Stanburys converted their hallway into a bar, the downstairs area into a plush lounge and dining room and redecorated the bedrooms one by one. The main attraction, ⁶.........., is still Jane's home cooking. The Stanbury's farmhouse hotel has just won a national award for Best Newcomer Hotel of the Year. Says Jane, 'We live in a lovely house. I just want to share it. I'm happy ⁷.......... people enjoy our home and our hospitality.'

4 Look at the example:

Life aboard ship is not without its *ups and downs*.

Now complete these sentences with the expressions below.

back to front   bed and breakfast   more or less
now and then   give and take   upside down

1 You can't have your own way all the time - you have to learn to ....
2 The guesthouse down the road charges £15.50 per night for ....
3 'How often do you see them?' 'Not often - just every ....
4 'What's wrong?' 'He didn't come right out and say it, but he .... accused me of lying.'
5 'Is this the right way up?' 'No, I think you've got it ....
6 Did you know you're wearing your jumper ....? Look, the pocket should be round the front.

5 Look at these expressions from the text in exercise 2 (page 11):

wide-brimmed hats   ankle-length dresses

Now match the compound adjectives in A with the nouns in B.

A	B
high-heeled	suit
an air-conditioned	decision
a double-breasted	ticket
front-page	actor
a part-time	news
a last-minute	shoes
a second-class	job
a world-famous	room

6 Revision

Use these phrases to write sentences about the Amish using *must*, *mustn't* and *don't have to*.

Example play cards - They *mustn't play* cards.

1 learn to drive a car ....
2 earn a lot of money..................................
3 maintain a simple way of life ....
4 buy a lot of clothes.................................
5 own a camera ....
6 avoid things that might corrupt them...............

7 PRACTICE SECTION

1 Complete these sentences by putting the verb in brackets in the correct form.

1 If he .... (*ask*) me to marry him, I'd accept.
2 If it rains, we .... (*cancel*) the match.
3 If you were ever unfaithful to me, I .... never .... (*forgive*) you.
4 If you .... (*try*), you could get a job.
5 If he .... (*call*), tell him I'm not here.
6 If you .... (*ask*) me for help, I'll help you.
7 What should I do if he .... (*not get*) a job?

2 Correct this letter with capital letters and punctuation marks.

dear sarah
two years ago my husband died people keep telling me that time heals but in fact i miss him more than ever i have no real friends in the area where i live and my relatives all live a long way away what can i do to stop my loneliness

....
....
....
....
....

3 Now complete the reply to the letter above with these words and phrases.

to face   try   I think you should   the best cure   great help

I'm glad you wrote to me, because talking to someone is a
¹.............................. I won't say that time heals, but with each passing year you will feel more able ²..............
.... people again. ³.............................. to find out if there are any evening classes in your area, and then ⁴.............................. enrol in a course that you would enjoy. This is a good way of meeting people, and is probably ⁵.............................. for your loneliness.

4 Complete the following tables.

Noun	Adjective
faithfulness	
honesty	
kindness	
tolerance	

Noun	Adjective
	lazy
	selfish
	loyal
	traditional
	shy
	stubborn
	generous

5 Write a description of your ideal partner. Write what he/she would look like, and say what personal qualities he/she would have.

....
....
....
....
....
....
....

6 Revision

Complete these sentences with *if* or *when*.

1 I'm expecting a call, so .... the telephone rings, would you answer it, please?
2 .... you're worried that someone is following you, walk to a police station.
3 'Is the report finished yet?' 'Not quite. I'll let you have it .... it's ready.'
4 .... I live to be 100, I'll get a telegram from the Queen.
5 Be careful! .... you drop that, it'll break.
6 Shall we go out .... you've finished your homework?

UNIT 8 PRACTICE SECTION

1
Join the pairs of sentences to answer the questions. Replace the word in italics with a relative pronoun. Then put brackets around the relative pronoun if it can be omitted.

Example Who's the man you were with? - He's a friend. I met *him* in France.
He's a friend (who) I met in France.

1 It's very unusual. What is it? - It's a necklace. I bought *it* in Egypt. ....

2 Why do you look so surprised? - I've just seen someone. I haven't seen *her* for years. ....

3 Why do you like her so much? - She's someone. I can talk to *her*. ....

4 What's wrong? - I've lost a ring. *It* belonged to my sister. ....

5 What's that old building in the photo? - That's the school. I used to attend *it* ....

6 Where are you living? - We're living in a cottage. *It* used to belong to my grandmother. ....

2
Use information from Unit 8 (page 15 - 16) and this table to write sentences.

| People who wear | a lot of / too much | red orange yellow green blue | may appear / seem | to be + adj |

Example People who wear a lot of red may appear to be aggressive.

3
Complete the text with these words.

behaviour   decorate ✓   experimented ✓   painted ✓   shade
tended to   very few

A university in England ¹................. with colour when the students decided to ²................. the dining room walls. They divided it into two rooms and painted one section a ³................. of red and the other section blue. Then the same food was served in the two rooms. ⁴................. students were aware of the experiment and the feedback was most interesting. In the blue room, the students ⁵................. speak softly, they thought the food was good and the room stayed clean. But in the room that was ⁶................. a shade of red, the students spoke more loudly, they thought the food was poor and the place quickly became untidy. This shows how far reaching the effects of colour on ⁷................. can be.

4
Change these nouns to adjectives and adverbs.

Noun	Adjective	Adverb
aggression	aggressive	aggressively
charm		
cheerfulness		
confidence		
energy		
independence		
joy		
optimism		
sadness		

5
For each sentence, replace the words in italics with one of the phrases below.

black and blue   ✓green with envy   have green fingers
off-colour   ✓out of the blue

1 'What happened?' 'I fell down the stairs. I'm *bruised* all over.'
2 'Were you expecting them to write?' 'No, the letter arrived completely *unexpectedly*.'
3 What a lovely garden. You must *be very good at gardening*.
4 'How are you?' 'Not very well. I feel a little *ill* today.'
5 When she won a four-week holiday in Spain, I felt *very jealous*.

6 Revision

Join these sentences using a non-defining relative clause. Replace the words in italics with a relative pronoun.

Example Nadia is very confident. *She* wears a lot of yellow.
Nadia, *who wears a lot yellow*, is very confident.

1 Green cars are not very popular. *They* are considered to be unlucky ....

2 Red roses are a popular gift. *They* are associated with love. ....

3 I have a red raincoat. I bought *it* in the sales. ....

4 Alan is very popular with women. *He* drives a yellow sports car. ....

5 Blue is my favourite colour. I wear *it* all the time ....

48

UNIT 9

PRACTICE SECTION

1 Look at a guest's list of complaints to the management of a hotel. Rewrite them in the passive voice. You don't need to use by + agent.

Example No one had cleaned my room before I checked in.
My room *hadn't been cleaned* before I checked in.

1 You'd promised me a view of the sea, ...
....

2 ... but you gave me a room facing the road. ....
....

3 You delivered my breakfast to the wrong room. ....
....

4 Someone stole my wallet while I was in the swimming pool ....

5 No one gave me fresh towels. ....
....

6 You'd closed the free health club and sauna the day before I arrived. ....

2 Match each of the sentences in A with the agent or doer in B.

A	B
1 John was arrested last night	a by the cleaners.
2 War and Peace was written	b by West Germany.
3 My house was robbed	c by the doctor.
4 My best coat was ruined	d by Tolstoy.
5 He was told that he had cancer	e by a thief.
6 Argentina was defeated in 1990	f by the police.

In which of the statements above is it not necessary to mention the agent?

3 Match the words and phrases in A with the definitions in B.

A	B
1 consumer	a A reduction in the usual price of something.
2 credit note	b A business that makes goods in large quantities.
3 discount	c Someone who buys things or uses the services.
4 manufacturer	d A piece of paper that proves you have paid for something
5 receipt	e Money that is returned to you because you have returned goods to a shop.
6 refund	f A piece of paper that states you can take goods up to a certain value from a shop without paying for them.

4 Read this letter of complaint. There are seven mistakes in it. Find and mark them in the following way:

G = grammar mistake   S = spelling mistake
P = punctuation mistake

64 High Street
Ashdown

The Manager
The Camera Shop
8 Dreighton Way
London

Dear Sir,

I am writing to you about a camera I have bought from your shop two weeks ago.
The first time I used the camera I discovered that the shutter was broke, I took the camera back to your shop imediately and asked to see the manager, but unfortunatly you were in a meeting. Since than I have been back to your shop twice, but both times I was told that you were not available. I will be returning to your shop on Monday at 11 am, at which time I would like to see you to return the camera. And to claim a full refund of my money.

Yours faithfully,

John Doe

5 Now write a similar letter to a jeweller's about a watch you bought which doesn't work. Use your own address and today's date. Make up the address of the jewellers where you bought the watch. Use the same layout and punctuation as the letter above.

6 Revision

Put the verbs in brackets in the correct tense - past simple or past perfect.

I ¹...*bought*... (*buy*) a new television set last month, and after I ²...*had used*... (*use*) it for a week, I ³...*discovered*... (*discover*) that it ⁴...*stopped*... (*stop*) working. I ⁵...*took*... (*take*) the television back to the shop where I ⁶...*had bought*... (*buy*) it and ⁷...*asked*... (*ask*) for my money back, but the manager ⁸...*refused*... (*refuse*) to give me a refund. He ⁹...*told*...... (*tell*) me that that the television ¹⁰...*had been*... (*be*) in good working order when they ¹¹...*had sold*...... (*sell*) it to me, and he ¹²...*offered*... (*offer*) to send it back to the manufacturer to be repaired.

49

UNIT 10 PRACTICE SECTION

1 For each sentence, use the word in brackets to give a reason. Use *because* and *because of*.

Example He had a car accident. (*careless*)
He had a car accident because he was careless.
                              because of his carelessness.

1 He failed his exams. (*lazy*) ....
....

2 People like her. (*generous*) ....
....

3 He failed his driving test. (*nervous*) ....
....

4 He doesn't have many friends. (*selfish*) ....
....

5 People trust him. (*honest*) ....
....

2 Rewrite these sentences using *because of*.

Example We cancelled the picnic because it was raining.
We cancelled the picnic *because of the rain*.

1 He got the job because he works hard. ....
....

2 I couldn't sleep because I had a pain in my chest. ....
....

3 I was late getting to work because there were traffic jams along the way. ....
....

4 The show closed after a week because the reviews were terrible. ....
....

5 We decided to stay at home because the weather was cold. ....
....

3 Complete the table, and then write sentences using words from the table and *make*.

Example Taking exams *makes me (feel) nervous*.

Cause	Effect
taking exams	nervous
drinking alcohol	....
studying	....
....	fat
....	ill
....	thirsty

Now write two more sentences of your own.

....
....

4 Which of these words go with *make* and which with *give*? Write them under the appropriate heading.

advice   a decision   an effort   an example   information
a mistake   progress   a promise   a reason   a noise
a speech   a talk

Make	Give
	advice

Now use a phrase beginning with *make* or *give* to complete each of the pairs of sentences.

1 I don't know what to do. Can you .... me some .... ?
2 Sssh. Be quiet! Don't ....
3 That's not right. You've ....
4 I don't know what to do. I can't ....
5 I don't understand what you mean. Can you ....
....?
6 I've tried hard. I've really ....

5 Work out the answers to these puzzles.

1 What is the sound of one hand clapping?
2 A man with a wooden leg lives on the 26th floor of a building. Every evening he gets into the lift on the ground floor, gets out of the lift on the 20th floor and walks up the remaining flights of stairs. Why does he do this?

6 Revision

Use these words and phrases to write sentences comparing people that you know.

aggressive   good at maths/languages   intelligent
intuitive   slim   tall

Example I am better at maths than my sister.

Yasuko is more aggressive than me. ✓
I am better at languages than my cousin.
.... is more intelligent than me.
My mother is more intuitive than me.
.... is more slimmer than me.
My boyfriend is taller than me.
....
....

UNIT 11

PRACTICE SECTION

1 Write one sentence saying what you have done at each of these places.

Example hairdresser's/barber's
   I *have my hair cut* at the hairdresser's.

1 garage ....
2 dentist's *I have my teeth examined at the dentist's*
3 eye doctor's *I have my eyes checked at the eye doctor's*
4 photographer's *I have my photos developed at the photographer's*
5 dry cleaner's *I had my clothes cleaned at the dry cleaner's*

2 Write sentences saying what these people *should/need to have done*. Use these words.

clean   cut   decorate   delivers   install   repair

Example Her car doesn't work. She *should have it repaired*.

1 Her jacket is dirty. *She should have it cleaned.*
2 Their house hasn't been painted for several years. *They should have it decorated*
3 Their grass is very long. *They should have it cut*
4 I need a second telephone. *I should have it installed*
5 I need some groceries, but I have no time to shop. *I should have delivered*

3 These words which appeared in the text in exercise 2 (page 21) can have other meanings. Use them to complete the sentences below.

arrange(ing)   duty   even   filed   irregular   pointed

1 Did you pay .... on those cigarettes when you came through customs?
2 His visits are so .... - we never know when to expect him.
3 You've done a wonderful job of .... the flowers.
4 'Where did you put those documents that were on my desk?' 'I .... them away yesterday.'
5 I was horrified when he .... a gun at me!
6 People with .... numbers stand on the right, please, and odd numbers stand on the left.

4 Complete the sentences below. Use a phrasal verb beginning with a form of *turn* and ending with one of these words. In each sentence, the phrasal verb should have a similar meaning to the word(s) in brackets.

back   down   in   off   on   over

1 I'm really tired. I think I'll .... (*go to bed*)
2 I asked him to marry me, but he .... me .... (*rejected*)
3 I .... the problem in my mind, but I couldn't find a solution. (*thought about*)
4 When it started to rain, we decided to .... (*return*)
5 We .... the main road, and proceeded down a path. (*left*)
6 Could you .... the heater, please. I'm cold. (*start working*)

5 Write a couple of paragraphs describing a festival or ceremony in your country. Include:

- when it is and why people celebrate it
- how people prepare for it
- how they celebrate it, eg food, clothing, activities

6 Revision

Complete the paragraph using the verbs below in the present simple passive.

build   haunt   hold   inhabit   perform   place   say

One festival in Hong Kong which is a major attraction for tourists is the Cheung Chau Bun Festival. The island of Cheung Chau [1]*is* now *inhabited* mainly by farmers and fishermen, but in the old days it was a centre for pirates. The festival [2].............. because the locals think that the island [3].............. by the ghosts of people who were killed by the pirates. The festival takes roughly a week, and in the final days of the festival, street operas [4].............. all over the island. A series of giant bamboo towers [5].............., on which the buns or cakes [6].............. These are rather hard sweet cakes with good luck inscriptions written on them. On the third day of the festival there is a huge scramble for the buns, because good luck [7].............. to come to anyone who is lucky enough to get one of the cakes and eat it.

UNIT 12 PRACTICE SECTION

1 Rewrite the sentences using the future perfect.

Example NASA plans to build a manned space station in the mid-nineties. - By the year 2000, NASA *will have built* a manned space station.

1 Many NASA senior employees are due to retire this year.
By the end of the year, ...
2 NASA plans to launch eighteen shuttles this year and next year.
By the end of next year, ...
3 They are going to send a telescope into space in 1990.
By 1991, ...
4 In the 1990s, they intend to build a space station on the moon.
By the 21st century, ...

2 Read the paragraph about Jenny's holiday plans.

Jenny is going to Greece for two weeks. She has arranged for a taxi to collect her from her house at 7.30 am. The taxi will take her to the airport. She will arrive at the airport at 8.30, check in and do her duty-free shopping. She will board the plane at 9.30 and at 9.45 her plane will depart. She will arrive in Athens at 1.00

Assume that there are no delays, and say what will have happened by these times.

7.40 By 7.40, the taxi will have collected her.

8.35 ....
9.15 ....
9.40 ....
10.00 ....
1.15 ....

3 Complete the article with a form of the word in brackets. Use one of these endings to change or complete that word.

-ent   -er   -ness   -ship   -ship   -ition   -tion

Space ace, 14, set for lift-off

Schoolgirl Helen Bridger has taken one small step towards becoming Britain's first woman astronaut at the age of 14. She has won a ¹................. (*scholar*) for a space shuttle course at the US Space and Rocket Centre in Huntsville, Alabama. For Helen, whose ²............... (*ambitious*) is to be the first woman to walk on the moon, it's a dream come true. She beat world-wide ³................ (*compete*) for the scholarship.
In an all-expenses paid whirlwind five days, Helen will simulate ⁴................. (*weightless*) in a huge tank of water. She will take command of the flight deck on a mock-up shuttle and assume the ⁵...............'s (*control*) role at command base.
Helen, a ⁶............... (*study*) at an all-girl grammar school, said 'I have dreamed of becoming an astronaut ever since I was old enough to have an ambition.'

The centre will pay for Helen's course, but she will have to find the airfare and she is hoping for ⁷..................... (*sponsor*).

4 Complete the sentences with some form of the word *back* and one of the words below.

car   streets   horse   form   wheels   door

1 Please sign your name on the .... of the ....
2 He .... the .... into the garage.
Fortunately, he stopped when he felt the ....
...... touch the bike which was in his path.
3 Could you come in through the .... please?
4 For once, he .... a winning .... and won quite a lot of money at the races.
5 He drove carefully through the narrow ....

5 Complete the tables with other forms of the words.

Adjective	Noun
exploding	....
enthusiastic	....
planetary	....
manned	....
confident	....

Verb	Noun
....	abandonment
multiply	....
develop	....
....	observatory
....	exploration

6 Revision

Complete the text. Write the verbs in brackets in the present perfect or past simple.

For centuries there ¹................. (*be*) reports of strange lights in the sky, space craft landing on earth and creatures coming out of them. As early as 1741, Lord Beauchamp ²................ (*see*) a small oval descend from the sky in England. It then ³................ (*disappear*). And in 1820, a stream of saucer-shaped objects ⁴............... (*fly*) across the town of Embrum, France. Recently, sightings of UFOs ⁵................. (*increase*). Some can be explained, but others remain mysteries.

UNIT 13

PRACTICE SECTION

1 Read the text and mark the statements as true or false - T or F. Correct the false statements.

One morning in May, an insurance salesman on his way to work on Wall Street, was standing near the open doors of a New York subway carriage that had stopped at a station.
A short, well-dressed man entered the carriage, bumped against the salesman, and left again. The insurance salesman instinctively felt for his wallet, found it missing, and reached out and grabbed the short man by his jacket collar. The subway doors closed with their rubber arms around the salesman's wrist, but he held on even after the train started moving. He managed to drag the other man several feet before the man's jacket tore, and the salesman was left holding the short man's collar in his hand.
Ten minutes after the insurance salesman arrived at his office, still angry, his wife called to tell him that he had left his wallet at home. (New York Times)

1 The insurance salesman was travelling to work on Wall Street. T/F
2 The short man entered the subway carriage and left again. T/F
3 The short man stole the salesman's wallet. T/F
4 The short man's jacket was torn before he entered the car. T/F
5 The salesman's wallet was safe at home. T/F

2 Now finish these statements about the incident on the subway.

1 If the short man hadn't bumped against the salesman, ..
....
2 If the salesman hadn't felt for his wallet, ...
....
3 If the salesman hadn't grabbed the short man's collar, ..
....
4 If the short man's jacket hadn't torn, ...
....
5 If the salesman hadn't left his wallet at home, ...
....

3 Write sentences about how your own life *would/might have been* different if you *had/hadn't done* certain things.

Example If I hadn't gone to university, I wouldn't have met my husband/wife.   If I had ..., I might have ...

....
....
....
....
....

4 Which of these words do you associate with success, with failure, or with neither? Write them under the best heading.

achievement   adequate   average   breakthrough
defeat   disappointment   flop   masterpiece   ordinary
prosperity   setback   mediocre

Success	Failure	Neither

What other words can you write under these headings?

5 Murphy's Law is a humorous rule that states that if something can go wrong, then it will. Match the first half of the Murphy's law statements in A with the second half in B.

A

1 The first place to look for something ...
2 Shoes in the sale ...
3 Whichever queue you join ...
4 Illnesses always ...
5 If you have the correct change for a pay phone ...
6 You never find something ...
7 If you take something back to a shop because it's faulty ...
8 If you're poor enough to need a bank loan, ...

B

a ... the one you find will be out of order.
b ... start on Friday.
c .1. is the last place you would expect to find it.
d ... you're too bad a risk to get one.
e ... the other one will always move faster.
f ... are never available in your size.
g ... until you've replaced it.
h ... it will work when you get it to the shop.

6 Revision

Write the verbs in brackets in the correct tense. Then say if the speaker thinks the event is possible or not probable.

Example If they *won* the next election, I think I'd leave the country. *not probable*

1 If I get my promotion, I .... (*take*) us all out to dinner to celebrate.
2 If I pass my English test, I .... (*register*) for the next course.
3 If I passed my driving test, I .... (*buy*) a new car.
4 If I .... (*have*) a better job, I'd earn more money.
5 If I .... (*live*) to be a hundred, I'll get a telegram from the Queen.

UNIT 14 PRACTICE SECTION

1 Change these statements from direct to indirect speech.

Example 'Colour comes from light,' said Newton. Newton said (that) colour comes/came from light.

1 'I'll tell you about my dream,' she said. ....
....

2 'It's late. I have to go,' she said. ....

3 'I'm living in London,' he said. ....
....

4 'They left on Saturday night,' he said. ....
....

5 'I've cut my finger,' she said. ....

6 'I'll be in Edinburgh on Thursday,' she said. ....
....

2 Read the woman's description of her dream. (Because there is only one speaker, you do not need to write *She said* in front of every sentence.)

1) 'In my dream, I can see people swimming, sailing and floating on the water.
2) The sun is shining and the people in the water are enjoying themselves.
3) I feel terrified because I can see a huge wave in the distance.
4) It's coming towards the people in the water.
5) I want to warn them, but I cannot speak.'
(One month later, a large wave swept over Sydney harbour. It killed several people.)

Complete the sentences below to report what she says in indirect speech.

1 She said that in her dream she could see ....
....

2 The sun ...., and the people...............
....

3 She said she .... because ....
....

4 The wave...

5 She said she ...., but she ....
....

3 Read the story about Mr Edwards who was admitted to hospital because the left side of his body was paralysed.

'The doctors told me they'd found a brain tumour that had paralysed the left side of my body. One night in hospital, I dreamed that someone was going to kill my dog, Rufus. I woke up with a cry and a big shock went through my left arm and leg. The nurses were absolutely amazed when I got out of bed and lifted up a chair. The doctors said that they had never seen anything like it. Six days after the nightmare, I was well enough to go home. It's my dog that cured me.'

Now rewrite these sentences in direct or indirect speech.

1 The doctor's told me they'd found a brain tumour that had paralysed the left side of my body.' The doctor's said, 'We've ....

2 'I dreamed that someone was going to kill my dog, Rufus.' Mr Edwards said that ....

3 'I woke up with a cry and a big shock went through my left arm and leg.' Mr Edwards said that ....

4 The doctors said that they had never seen anything like it. The doctors said, 'We ....

5 'It's my dog that cured me.' Mr Edwards said ....
....

4 Which word doesn't belong in each of the sets of words below? Why?

a order	command	remark	insist
b begin	reply	respond	answer
c cry	shout	shriek	say
d argue	assert	plead	insist
e whisper	cry	mutter	mumble
f ask	state	inquire	question
g inquire	say	state	declare

5 Use these words to complete the story about Sugar Ray Robinson, the champion boxer.

assured   do   of   of   the   they   to   with

A dream that came true despite the dreamer's efforts [1]...... change the course of destiny happened in 1947, in [2]....... boxing ring. Just before Sugar Ray Robinson's title fight [3]........ Jimmy Doyle, Robinson dreamed that during the fight, one [4]...... his punches killed Doyle. Robinson's manager and his priest [5].......... him that dreams simply did not come true. But [6]..........were wrong. They should have told him that dreams [7]....... not always come true. In the eighth round, one [8]........ Robinson's punches killed Jimmy Doyle.

6 Revision

Complete the table. Show the tense change from indirect to direct speech.

Indirect	Direct
did	do/does
was/were doing	....
had done	....
was going to do	....
would	....
could	....

54

UNIT 15

PRACTICE SECTION

1 Look at these facts about Joe's life and match what he intended to do in A with what really happened in B.

A	B
1 leave school at 16	a stayed in London
2 travel around the world alone	b bought a house
	c fell in love and got married
3 study to be a policeman	d parents convinced him to finish his university education
4 move to Canada	e wife convinced him to become a lawyer
5 buy a sports car	

Now join the phrases in A and B to make sentences. Use *was going to* and *but*.

Example He was going to leave school at sixteen, but his parents convinced him to finish his education.

2 Imagine yourself in these situations. For each situation, write at least three things you wish you had/hadn't done.

1 You are in a foreign country. You book into a cheap hotel with poor security. You put all your money and your important papers in your bag, and leave the bag in your hotel room when you go down to breakfast. When you go back to your room, you discover that someone has stolen the bag.

2 You went to a party last night. You drank too much and stayed up very late. You have an important business meeting today. You feel ill and very tired.

3 A stranger asks you to take a small suitcase to another country for them. You agree. You are stopped at Customs and the suitcase is opened. It is full of drugs.

4 You have decided to walk home from a friend's house late at night. It has started to rain, and you are wet and cold. You have lost your way, and you think someone might be following you.

3 Write three sentences about things you *were going to do* but didn't. Give your reason for not doing those things.

Example I was going to study art, but I changed my mind.

....
....
....

Then write three sentences about things you wish you had/hadn't done in your life.

Example I wish I'd studied law. I wish I hadn't got married.

....
....
....

4 Use these words to complete the story.

an   be   do   for   I   let   not   now   of   the
to   told   was   were

The Hawk and the Nightingale

A nightingale was sitting alone among the branches of ¹..... oak tree. She was singing beautifully and the woods ²..... filled with her song. Not far away, a hawk ³..... searching the woods for something to eat. He heard ⁴..... nightingale, swooped down, caught her in his talons, and ⁵..... her to prepare to die. 'Oh,' said the nightingale, '⁶..... not kill me. I never did anything wrong - and ⁷..... am so small I would only be a mouthful ⁸..... you. Why don't you attack a larger bird, and ⁹..... me go?' 'Yes,' said the hawk, 'you may try ¹⁰..... persuade me to let you go. But I had ¹¹..... found any prey today until I saw you. And ¹²..... you want me to let you go in hope ¹³..... finding something better? If I did that, who would ¹⁴..... the fool?'

5 These are the words for describing parts of a house, but the letters are jumbled. Put the letters in the right order to make words. Then use the words to label the picture.

hmcniye   ofor   lciengi   dghee   ncefe   diwnow
teag   odro   tpsse   isrtas   pfrieclea

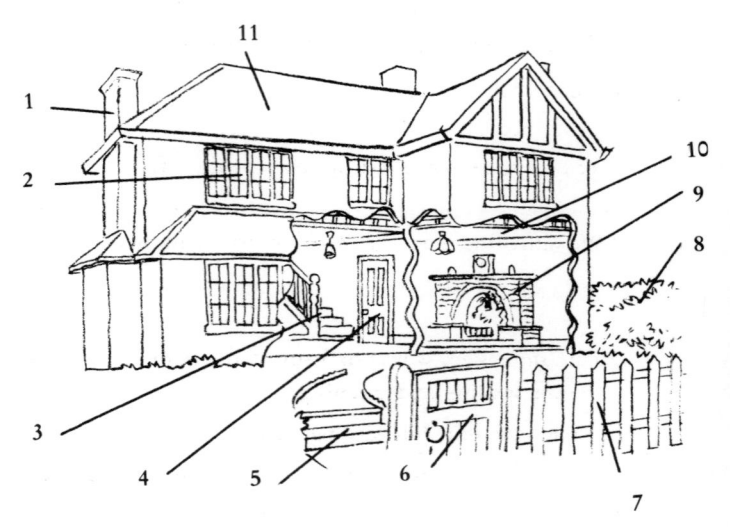

6 Revision

Use *will* or *going to do* to complete the short dialogues.

1 'The phone's ringing!' 'I .... answer it.'
2 'Are you and Susan engaged?' 'Yes, we .... get married in the spring.'
3 'Your new house needs a lot of work.' 'I know. We .... start work on it next year, when we can afford it.'
4 'Have you rung for a taxi yet?' 'No, I forgot. I .... ring for one now.'
5 'What are your plans for this evening?' 'I .... study for my exam tomorrow.'

UNIT 16 PRACTICE SECTION

1 Rewrite these sentences with *unless*.

Example If you don't work harder, you'll fail your exams.
You'll fail your exams *unless you work harder*.

1 If we don't leave right now, we'll miss the beginning of the performance. ....
....

2 If you don't see a doctor soon, you're going to end up in hospital. ....
....

3 If we don't begin to respect the earth, we're going to have terrible problems. ....
....

4 If you don't slow down, you'll have an accident. ....
....

2 Rewrite each of the sentences so that the second sentence means the same as the first.

1 You must be there on time, or I'll leave without you.
If ....
....

2 You must practise, or you will never learn to drive.
Unless. ....
....

3 You must get some rest or you'll be ill. If. ....
....

4 We must ring them, or they'll worry. Unless. ....
....

3 Homophones are words that sound the same but have a different spelling and meaning.

Example I can *hear* him singing. He's over *here*.

Complete the sentences with a homophone of one of these words.

sun   rain   weather   sea   flower

1 I don't know .... he's here or not.
2 It was the during the .... of Elizabeth I that Britain defeated the Spanish Armada.
3 I must go to the shop. I'm out of .... and eggs.
4 We've got four children, but Andrew is our only ....
....
5 Can you clean the windscreen, please. I can't ....
where I'm going.

4 Match the questions in A with an appropriate response in B.

A
1 Beautiful weather we're having.
2 What's the weather like in your country?
3 What's the temperature?
4 Is it still raining?
5 What's the forecast for tomorrow?
6 What awful weather!
7 Is your country humid?

B
a No, it's very dry.
b No, it's just stopped.
c They say it's going to snow.
d It's sunny and warm most of the year
e It's 23 degrees.
f Yes, isn't it lovely.
g I know. Isn't it terrible.

5 Complete the text with these words.

as   big   his   only   so   State   the   times   times

Lightning always takes the quickest path to the ground, ¹..............
tall trees and buildings are most at risk. The Empire ²............... Building, in New York, has been hit as much ³.............. twelve times in twenty minutes, and as often as 500 ⁴.......... a year. Lightning does not often strike people. However, ⁵......... only person to survive being struck by lightning seven ⁶............ was an American, Roy C. Sullivan. He lost his ⁷..........toenail in 1952, his eyebrows in 1969, and had ⁸.........
hair set on fire twice. The other times he suffered ⁹.........
.... minor burns.

6 Revision

In the next century, do you think there will be:

1 a single world government? ....
....

2 more/less pollution? ....
....

3 colonies on other planets? ....
....

4 cities under the water? ....
....

5 a cure for AIDS? ....
....

Write sentences expressing your opinions. Use (*definitely*) *will/won't*, *will probably*, *may* or *probably won't*.

Example I don't think there will /There probably won't be a single world government.

56

UNIT 17 PRACTICE SECTION

1 Imagine a doctor has asked you these questions. Write them as indirect questions.

Example How old are you?
The doctor asked me how old I was.

1 Did you have any breakfast? *The doctor asked if I had any breakfast.*
2 How are you feeling? *The doctor asked how I am feeling.*
3 When did you first notice the swelling? *The doctor asked when you first noticed the swelling.*
4 Are you experiencing any pain? *The doctor asked if I am experience any pain.*
5 How long have you had the rash? *The doctor asked how long I have had the rash.*

2 The doctor's orders and advice to a patient are in italics. Write them as indirect speech. Use *advised* or *told* as your reporting verbs.

a) *Roll up your sleeve*. That's right. I want to take your blood pressure. Now, just b) *relax*. Right, your blood pressure is far too high. First of all, c) *you need to take regular exercise*. Oh, and d) *you should also give up smoking*. And e) *you need to eat a sensible diet*, as well. And, of course, you should avoid unnecessary stress - f) *don't work too hard*. Oh, and g) *come and see me in a week*.

Example a The doctor told the patient to roll up his sleeve.
b *The doctor advised him to be relax.*
c *The doctor told him to take regular exercise.*
d *The doctor advised him to give up smoking.*
e *The doctor told him to eat a sensible diet.*
f *The doctor advised me not to work too hard.*
g *The doctor told him to see him in a week.* (come and)

3 Where possible, write the direct object *me* in the space after the reporting verb.

1 Alex told .... that he wasn't well.
2 The doctor asked .... to come in and shut the door.
3 Yvonne said ...... that she would like to go to the theatre.
4 She asked .... how I was feeling.
5 She said .... to buy some tickets.
6 She asked .... if I had been taking my medicine.
7 He told .... not to tell anyone.

In which two sentences is the use of *me* optional?

4 Complete the sentences. Use *come* in the correct tense and one of the words/phrases below to form a phrasal verb that is similar in meaning to the word/phrase in brackets.

in for   out in   for   through

1 Ian .... a terrible rash. (*was covered with*)
2 He .... me with a knife. I thought he was going to kill me. (*threatened to attack*)
3 The government's policies have .... a lot of criticism lately. (*received*)
4 How is he? Fine, he has .... the operation very well. (*survived*)

5 Ian had great difficulty walking. It was all he could do to *hobble* to hospital.

Which of these words is nearest in meaning to the word *hobble*: march, limp, stroll?

In English, there are often many different ways to express one general meaning, eg to walk. Complete these sentences using the verbs below in the correct form.

march   stroll   stride   jog   chase   waddle

1 The army .... into army territory.
2 It was Sunday afternoon, and a couple were .... arm in arm through the park.
3 Don't let that dog .... the cat through the flower garden!
4 I like to .... three times a week for exercise.
5 The models .... into the room, displaying their designer dresses.
6 The fat man .... into the room, and then settled himself in the nearest chair.

How many other words can you think of to describe different ways of walking?

6 Revision

Complete each sentence with a form of one of these words.

admit   argue   beg   complain   suggest   threaten   warn

1 She was very upset. She .... me not to tell anyone her secret.
2 She.................... of a pain in her side, so I took her to see a doctor.
3 Alan ....his case very well, I thought. He certainly convinced me.
4 They .... we meet them for a drink this evening. What do you think?
5 They .... that they had made a mistake.
6 Alice .... him to leave her alone. In fact, she .... to call the police if he didn't.

UNIT 18 PRACTICE SECTION

1 Say what *could/might/may have happened* in these situations. For each situation, write one or two sentences.

1 You arranged to meet a friend outside the cinema at half past eight. It is now five past nine. What could have happened?

Example He/She could have forgotten. ....
....

2 At the bank, you try to cash a cheque. You think you have plenty of money, but the clerk tells you your account is empty...
....

3 It's late at night. In the house next door, you hear people shouting. Several minutes later, an ambulance arrives. ...
....
....

2 Read the story of the Mary Celeste and put the parts of the text a - e in the correct order..

a She was adrift and the captain and the crew of the Dei Gratia were amazed to find that the Mary Celeste had been abandoned - there was no trace whatsoever of her captain and crew. The ship's lifeboat and some of her navigational instruments were missing, but everything else was in place.
b Any of these events would have left evidence of damage or struggle, and there was none. In the end, the investigators had to admit they didn't know what had happened.
c The mystery of the Mary Celeste has fascinated historians for over a century. The story of the ill-fated ship is this: On November 5 1872, the Mary Celeste set sail from New York. On December 5 a second ship, the Dei Gratia, encountered the Mary Celeste off the coast of Portugal.
d Many explanations for the disappearance have been offered, but to this day, the Mary Celeste remains one of the great unsolved mysteries of the sea.
e A search was begun for the captain and crew but they were never found. What is more, no reason could be found for them to abandon the ship. All the usual reasons - storms, pirate attack, mutiny - were considered and discarded.

3 Write sentences about what *might have happened* to the captain and crew of the Mary Celeste.

Example They might have jumped overboard.
They might have swum away..................
....
....

4 These are Mr Pagett's answers to some of Inspector Finch's questions. Write the questions.

Example About an hour ago. - *When did you arrive from London?*

1 By car..
2 In front of the hotel................................
3 I manage the family business ....
4 Yes, we're very happy ....

Now write three more questions that Inspector Finch might have asked one of the other suspects.

5 Use the words below to complete the paragraph.

arrest   trial   court   guilty   evidence   innocent
sentence   accused

When a crime is committed, the police must first look for ¹... evidence .... and compile a list of suspects. When they think they have found the person responsible for the crime, they ²... arrest ...... him or her. When a person is ³.... accused ..... of a crime, they may have to go to prison to await ⁴... trial ...... Eventually they go to ⁵. court ...... and it is decided if they are ⁶. innocent ... or ⁷... guilty ..... If they are found innocent, they are released. But if they are found guilty, then the judge will ⁸. sentence .... them.

6 Revision

Look at the outline of Joe's life of crime.

1968	- leaves school at the age of 14
	- can't find a job because he's too young
	- starts breaking into houses to make money
1974	- robs a bank of a million pounds
	- hides the money before he is captured
1975	- goes to prison
1980	- escapes from prison
	- gets the money and goes to South America
1990	- falls in love with an English tourist there
	- flies back to Britain to see her
	- re-captured by police and discovers his girlfriend is an undercover police officer

Now finish these sentences and say what *would/might (not) have happened.*

Example If he had left school at 16 he might have found a job.

1 If he had found a job,..............................
....

2 If he hadn't robbed a bank of £1,000,000, ...
....

3 If he hadn't hidden the money, ...
....

Now write the first part of these sentences.

4 ...., he wouldn't have flown back to Britain.
5 ...., he wouldn't have been re-captured by the police.
6 ...., he would still be living in South America.

58

UNIT 19 PRACTICE SECTION

1 Look at the pictures of the Desert Hotel before and after new management took it over. Write sentences about what has been done to the hotel under the new management. Use these verbs.

build   paint   plant   repair   install

Example The sign has been repaired.

2 Look at these phrases from the text on Palmyra:

pri... (...sive) silk and jade
vast ... erts

Complete ... nces. Use the strong adjectives below to rep... in brackets. One of the adjectives can be used ...

brilliant   ...   furious   heart-breaking
hilarious   ...nute

1 He told a(n) .... joke. (*very funny*)
2 The film is a(n) .... story. (*very sad*)
3 He flicked a switch and the room was filled with .... light. (*very bright*)
4 There was a(n) .... amount of poison in the drink, but it was enough to kill him. (*very small*)
5 I've just had a(n) .... idea. (*very clever*)
6 They live in a(n) .... house. (*very large*)
7 I've never seen him like that - he was .... (*very angry*)

3 Where would you expect to find these animals? Match the animals in A with the places that they inhabit in B.

A	B
1 camel	a savannah
2 brown bear	b ice sheet
3 monkey	c desert
4 whale	d ocean
5 giraffe	e prairie
6 penguin	f jungle
7 buffalo	g forest

4 Complete each of the sentences with one of these prepositions:

at   in   of   on   to

1 I live ..... London.
2 They have moved .... Birmingham.
3 They've just bought a house ...... the north of England.
4 My house is ...... the corner, next to the post office.
5 Turn left .... the traffic lights and you can't miss it.
6 Palmyra is a city ...... the Syrian desert.
7 Look ...... your right and you'll see the museum.
8 They live ...... 32 Westland Drive.

5 Write a description of your city or country. Write about:

location   climate   interesting things to see or do there
what you like/dislike about it

....
....
....
....
....
....
....
....

6 Revision

Why do you go to these places? What do you have done there? Answer using *to have something done*.

Example I go to a tailor/seamstress ...
I go to a tailor *to have a suit made*.

1 I go to a heel bar. ....
2 I go to a dry cleaner's ....
3 I go to a manicurist ....
4 I go to a fortune-teller ....
5 I go to a jeweller's ....

59

UNIT 20

PRACTICE SECTION

See exercise 3 (page 39). Add up your scores and then read the result of your quiz.

Scores 1 a = 3, b = 4, c = 1, d = 2
2 a = 3, b = 4, c = 2, d = 1
3 a = 2, b = 3, c = 4, d = 1
4 a = 4, b = 2, c = 3, d = 1
5 a = 4, b = 3, c = 2, d = 1
6 a = 4, b = 3, c = 1, d = 2

6 - 10 You think you'd make a great leader, but in reality you might not. On the positive side, you can see other people's strong points easily. But you can be bossy and you don't always listen to other people. Good leaders are natural listeners and helpers as well as directors.

11 - 15 You might make a good leader. You're sensible and can often see the way to solve problems before others. But you tend to get very emotional about things. Leaders should approach day-to-day problmes coolly, which is what you should do - a little more thought and less emotion, please.

16 - 20 You're a born leader. You're strong and can assert yourself. Also, you're interested in people and take time to get to know them. But you're not worried about people liking you all the time - you basically do what you know is right. You know how to encourage people when they do something well rather than criticise them when they make a mistake.

21 - 24 You prefer to follow the crowd, but this means that you sometimes put up with things that you shouldn't. It's all right to be a follower, as long as you follow the right people. On the positive side, you're a kind person. But sometimes a little rebellion can go a long way. Leaders don't always follow the rules - their instincts are better judges.

1 Which of the following are characteristics of a good leader? Compare your answers with the text above.

1 likes helping people
2 tends to get emotional
3 doesn't listen to other people
4 is assertive
5 wants to be liked all the time
6 trusts his/her instincts

2 Read the extract from an article on President John F Kennedy. Complete the text with *a*, *an* or *the*.

It was ¹..... morning of Friday, 22 November, 1963. ²..... President was riding in ³..... open-top limousine through Dallas, Texas. His wife, Jacqueline, was next to him. ⁴..... Texas governor and his wife were in ⁵..... front seat. ⁶..... crowds were cheering wildly. ⁷..... limousine turned left in front of ⁸..... seven-storey building called ⁹..... Texas School Book Depository. Shots rang out. ¹⁰..... President slumped over. He was taken to hospital, but efforts to save him failed. His death was announced at 1.33 local time. ¹¹..... world was stunned. Kennedy's death gave America ¹²..... martyr. He instantly became ¹³..... great president. Even now, people in Europe and America still consider him one of ¹⁴..... greatest leaders of ¹⁵..... century.

3 Complete the sentences with *a*, *an* or *the*.

1 She won ..... Best Actress award last year.
2 In hot countries, people often sleep in ..... afternoon.
3 'Can you help me?' 'I'm afraid I'm busy at ..... moment.'
4 Can you give me ..... moment of your time?
5 We went to ..... most expensive restaurant in town.
6 Meet me at ..... church at 7.00 pm.
7 'What do you do?' 'I'm ..... teacher.'
8 He plays ..... guitar beautifully.
9 The journey took us ..... hour.

4 In each of the sentences, write *a* or *an* in front of the word in italics where it is needed to make the sentence grammatical.

1 I think we should try to enjoy *life*, don't you?
2 Have you ever saved *life*?
3 *Paper* comes from trees.
4 Could you get me *paper* at the newsagent's, please?
5 *Dog* will be your friend for life.
6 *Dogs* make good companions.

5 Match the words with the definitions.

1 captain	a	someone who is in charge of a newspaper or magazine
2 editor	b	someone who is in charge of a ship or a sports team
3 general	c	someone who holds a very high rank in an army
4 matron	d	someone who organises plays or films
5 president	e	someone who is the leader of a country or organisation
6 producer	f	someone who is in charge of the nurses in a hospital

6 Revision

Fill in the gaps in the text with the words below.

by   tear   started   the   souvenir   yesterday   it   his

Reagan hammers out his message

Ronald Reagan hammered away at ¹..... remnants of the Berlin Wall ²............
As he chipped out a ³............, the former US president said '⁴..... feels great.'
Shielded by bodyguards, Mr Reagan and his wife Nancy ⁵..... an 11-day tour of Europe ⁶..... walking through East Berlin's Brandenburg Gate.
This was the back-drop for ⁷..... 1987 challenge to Mikhail Gorbachev to '⁸......... down this wall'.

Grammar reference

Unit 1

infinitive of purpose

1. When you want to talk about the purpose of an action, you can use a clause beginning with *to*-infinitive.
   They were shoving each other out of the way *to get* to the front.
   The children sleep together *to keep* warm

2. You cannot use a negative with a *to*-infinitive purpose clause. For example, you cannot say:
   *We keep the window shut not to let the flies in.
   You would have to say:
   We keep the window shut *in order not to let* the flies in.

Unit 2

gerunds as subjects and objects

1. Gerunds, or *-ing* words, are nouns that have the same form as the present participle of a verb.
   running   walking   going

2. They are used to refer to an activity, action or process in a general way.
   Running is an excellent form of exercise.
   Because gerunds refer to activities in a general way, they are usually uncountable nouns: that is, they have only one form, they cannot be used with numbers, and they do not usually have a determiner (*the*, *a*, or *an*) in front of them.

3. Because they act like nouns, gerunds can act as subjects or objects of a verb.
   Singing is one of my interests. - **subject** of a verb
   I love *dancing*. - **object** of a verb

Unit 3

who and which to give extra information

1. Non-defining relative clauses give extra information that is not needed to identify the person or thing you are talking about.
   Sir Denis, *who is 78*, let it be known that ... **non-defining**
   I met the woman *who lives next door*. **defining**
   Note that you put the relative clause immediately after the noun which refers to the person, thing or group that you are talking about.

2. When you are referring to people, you use *who* as the subject of a non-defining clause, and *who* or *whom* as the object of a non-defining clause. *Whom* is rarely used.
   Heath, *who died in 1944*, was a cartoonist. **subject**
   That's one of the things that Heath, *who(m) I do not like*, had a clear idea about. **object.**

3. When you are referring to a thing or group of things, you use *which* as the subject or object of a non-defining clause.
   The treatment, *which is being tried by researchers*, has ...

4. A non-defining relative clause usually has a comma in front of it and a comma after, unless it comes at the end of the sentence, in which case you use a comma before the clause and a full stop at the end.

5. Relative clauses are much more usual in written English than in spoken English.

Unit 4

present perfect or past simple?

1. If you want to mention something that happened in the past, but you do not want to mention a specific time, you use the present perfect.
   The local council *have raised* £180 for a swimming pool.
   However, if you then say more about the event, the past simple is normally used:
   They *raised* the money through ...
   If you want to say that an event occurred or that something was the case at a definite time in the past, you use the past simple.
   The Prime Minister *flew* into New York yesterday ...

3. You cannot use words or phrases that place an event at a definite time in the past with the present perfect. However, you can use phrases which show duration, or which show that the action is repeated.
   They have left the area *forever*.
   I have *often* criticised the standards of cleanliness ...

4. When you are talking about a quality, attitude or possession that still exists, you must use the present perfect with a word or phrase to show duration.
   We've had it *for* fifteen years.
   He's *always* liked you, you know.

Unit 5

adverbs of manner

1. Adverbs of manner give more information about the way in which an action or event takes place.
   He smiled *warmly*.

2. The position of adverbs within sentences is flexible. They are normally placed after the verb group or after the object or complement if there is one.
   She packed *carefully*.
   However, for emphasis, you can place the adverb at the beginning of the sentence.
   Carefully, she made her way down the stairs.
   Adverbs can also be placed between the subject and the main verb. This position puts more emphasis on the adverb than when it is after the verb group, but not as much as putting it at the beginning of the sentence.

GRAMMAR REFERENCE

I *carefully* made my way down the stairs.

3 After verbs of perception (*looks, sounds, tastes, feels, smells*) you use *good* rather than *well*.

She sings *well*.

That sounds *good*.

by + -ing

You can use a gerund after *by* to show how something happened or to describe how someone did something.

The prisoners escaped from prison *by digging a tunnel*.

Unit 6

permission

1 *Not allowed/permitted* can also be used to show that something is forbidden because of a rule or a law.

You are *not allowed/permitted to* enter. **Formal**

2 You can also use *forbidden* to talk about negative or refused permission. You do not need another negative word because the word itself has a negative meaning.

Walking on the grass *is forbidden*. **passive**

obligation

1 If you say that something is (*not*) *supposed* to be done, you mean that it should or shouldn't be done because of a rule, law or custom.

You're *supposed to* report an accident to the police.

You're *not supposed to* park your car on the motorway.

2 To say that something is required or expected because it is the correct thing to do, you can use *should* or *ought to*.

We *should send* them a postcard.

We *ought to stay* with him.

3 To say that something is required by a rule or a law, you can use *must*:

You *must apply* within six months.

Unit 7

first and second conditional

1 When you want to talk about a possible situation and its consequences, you use a conditional clause. Conditional clauses usually begin with *if* or *unless*.

2 Learners of English are often taught that there are three kinds of conditional sentences: first, second and third. This is largely correct, but it does not fully describe all the types of conditional sentences that are possible.

3 There are special rules about which tense to use in conditional sentences. Some of these rules are:

a) When you are talking about a possible future occurrence, you use the simple present in the conditional clause and the simple future in the main clause. (This is often referred to as the first conditional.)

If I ever *get* out of this alive, I*'ll* never *leave* you again.

b) When you are talking about an unlikely situation, you use the simple past in the conditional clause and *would*, *should* or *might* in the main clause. (This is often referred to as the second conditional.)

They *would find* it difficult to get a job if they *left* the farm.

I *should be* surprised if it *was* less than five pounds.

Note that *were* is sometimes used instead of *was* especially after *I*. *If I were you ...* as a way of giving advice is a variation of this pattern.

If I were you, I'd accept him as he is.

Note that when you are talking about a common occurrence, you use the simple present or the present continuous in the conditional clause and in the main clause. (This pattern is often referred to as the zero conditional.)

If a man *looks* at me, I *am* flattered.

Unit 8

pronouns in defining relative clauses

1 Defining relative clauses explain which person or thing you are talking about. For example, if you say:

I met the woman.

it is not clear who you are talking about unless you say:

I met the woman *who lives next door*.

In this sentence, *who lives next door* is a defining relative clause. You never put a comma or a dash in front of a defining relative clause.

2 When you are referring to a person or group of people, you use *who* or *that* as the subject of a defining clause. *Who* is more common than *that*.

I know the people *who live in this cottage*.

3 You use *who, that* or *whom* as the object of a defining clause or you do not use a pronoun at all.

She's someone (*who(m)/that*) *I haven't seen for a long time*.

4 When you are referring to a thing or group of things, you use *which* or *that* as the subject of a defining clause.

There are a lot of things *that are wrong*.

5 You use *which* or *that* as the object of a defining clause, or you do not use a pronoun at all.

One of the things (*which/that*) *I'll never forget* is ...

6 A relative pronoun can be the object of a preposition. Usually the preposition goes towards the end of the clause and not in front of the pronoun.

.... the universe (*which/that*) *we live in*.

Unit 9

the passive

1 Passive forms consist of the verb *be* in the same tense as the active verb followed by the past participle of the active verb.

Someone *gave* him the letter yesterday. **active**

He *was given* the letter yesterday. **passive**

Clauses containing an active form of the verb are in active voice and clauses containing a passive are in passive voice.

GRAMMAR REFERENCE

2 Using a passive form of a verb gives you the option of not mentioning the person or thing responsible for the action, often called the agent of the action. You may want to do this for one of these reasons:
a) because you do not know who or what the agent is.
b) because it is not important who or what the agent is.
c) because it is obvious who or what the agent is.
d) because the agent has already been mentioned.
e) because people in general are the agents.
f) because you wish to conceal the agent's identity or to distance yourself from the action.

3 When you use the passive, you can of course mention the agent at the end of the clause by using *by*. This puts emphasis on the agent because the end of the clause is an important position, and so you often do this when you want to refer back to the agent in the next clause.
   His best friend was killed *by a grenade, which exploded under his car.*

Unit 10
because and *because of*

1 When you want to indicate the reason for something, you use a reason clause. The main conjunctions used in reason clauses are: *as, because (of), in case, just in case* and *since*.

2 You use *because (of), since* or *as* if you are simply indicating the reason for something. After *because of* you must use a noun, a gerund or a noun phrase.
   I couldn't feel angry *because* I liked him so much.
   because of liking him so much.
   Note that you use *in case* or *just in case* when you are mentioning a possible future situation which is someone's reason for doing something. You use the simple present in the reason clause.
   I'll take a coat *in case it rains.*

make
1 You use *make* when the cause is the subject of the sentence. After *make* and the direct object, you can use either an adjective or an infinitive.
   Writing exams *makes me nervous.*
   Listening to classical music *makes me want* to go to sleep.

Unit 11
have something done

1 A special use of *have* is to say that the subject causes something to be done or dealt with by someone else. In this case, *have* is followed by an object referring to the thing dealt with, and then by the past participle of a verb.
   He went to *have his teeth checked.*

2 This structure is also used to say that something belonging to the subject is affected in some way.
   She *had her money stolen.*

3 If you want to mention the performer of the action, you use *by* followed by a noun (group).
   He had his eyes checked *by the doctor.*

4 *Get* can also be used with an object and a past participle in a similar way to *have*.
   We must *get the car repaired.*

Unit 12
future perfect

1 The future perfect is formed by using *will* or *shall*, followed by *have* and the past participle of the main verb.
   Long before you return, they *will have forgotten* you.

2 The future perfect is sometimes called the past in the future. You use the future perfect if you are referring to something that has not happened yet, but will happen before a particular time in the future.
   The concert *will have started* by the time we get there.

3 The future perfect is often used with a time adverbial beginning with *by*.
   By the year 2000, we'll have found a cure for cancer.

Unit 13
third conditional

1 You use the third conditional when you are talking about something that might have happened in the past, but did not happen.

2 In third conditional sentences, the verb in the main clause is *would have* or *should have*, and the verb in the conditional clause is in the past perfect. (*Would* and *had* are often shortened to *'d*.)
   If she *had not married*, she *would have had* a great career.

3 You can also use *could have* or *might have* in the main clause.

Unit 14
direct and indirect speech

1 When you report what somebody has said or thought using your own words rather than the words they actually used, you use indirect or reported speech.
   He thought she was worried.

2 When you use indirect speech, you are usually reporting something that was said or believed in the past. Both the reporting verb and the verb in the reported clause are therefore usually in a past tense.
   In the Middle Ages, people *thought* the world *was* flat.

3 You can use a present tense of the reporting verb:
a) when you are reporting something that someone says or believes at the time of speaking.
   Experts *say* you should be accurate.
b) when you are reporting something said in the past that

GRAMMAR REFERENCE

someone often says or that is still true.

My doctor *says* it's nothing to worry about.

4 Whatever the tense of the reporting verb, you should put the verb in the reported clause in a tense that is appropriate at the time that you are speaking:

a) When the reporting verb is in a past tense, a past tense is also usually used for the verb in the reporting clause, even if the reported situation still exists.

He said he *was* English.

I told him I *was* 18.

However a present tense is sometimes used to stress that the situation still exists.

I told him that I *don't drink* more than anyone else.

b) If the event was in the past when the reported statement was made, you use the past simple or past perfect.

She said that she *enjoyed/had enjoyed* the course.

c) If the situation described in the reported clause is in the past at the time of speaking, you use the simple past, the past continuous or the present perfect.

Dad explained that he *had* no money.

She added that she *was smoking* too much.

He says he *has* never *seen* a live shark in his life.

5 Modals in indirect speech:

a) when you want to report someone's ability to do something, you use *could*.

They thought they *could* help him

b) when you want to report a prediction or a promise, you use *would*.

She said they *would* miss us.

Unit 15

I wish I'd

1 You can use *wish* + past perfect to talk about past actions or events that you regret happened or didn't happen.

I *wish I'd studied* law.

I *wish I hadn't left* school when I was 16.

2 Other ways of expressing regret are *If only I'd done ..., then ...*

If only I hadn't left school early, I'd be rich by now.

Note that *wish* is also used to express a desire for change.

I *wish you'd stop* telling me what to do!

was/were going to

1 *Was/Were going to* is used to talk about an event which a) was in the future at a particular time in the past, b) was thought to be going to occur. The implication is usually that the event did not take place.

2 A clause containing *was/were going to* is often followed by a clause beginning with *but*, which explains why the first event did not take place.

I *was going to travel* to Europe, *but* my family didn't want me to go.

Unit 16

unless

1 Conditional clauses usually begin with *if* or *unless*. *Unless* means *if ... not*. For example:

You will fail your exams *unless you work harder*.

means:

If you do not work harder, you will fail your exams.

2 Sentences with *unless* are often used when you are warning someone about the possible consequences of an act or situation.

3 Clauses beginning with *unless* usually go after a main clause. However, if you want to make a warning stronger, you often put the *unless* clause at the beginning of the sentence.

Unit 17

indirect questions

1 The reporting verb most often used for indirect questions is *ask*.

2 When you report a question a) you do not treat it as a question by using interrogative word order b) you do not use a question mark.

3 There are two main types of questions, and so two main types of report structure for questions.

a) When you report a question that can be answered by *yes/no* you use a clause beginning with *if* or *whether*.

She asked him *if his parents spoke French*.

I asked him *whether he agreed*.

b) When you report a wh-question, you use a 'wh' word at the beginning of the clause.

He asked *where I was going*.

She inquired *why I was so late*.

I asked *how they liked the film*.

indirect orders

1 If someone orders, requests or advises someone else to do something, this can be reported by using a *to*-infinitive clause after a reporting verb such as *tell*. The person being addressed is mentioned as the object of the reporting verb.

I *told her to wake* me *up*.

He *ordered me to fetch* the books.

The doctor *advised me to see* a specialist.

2 In ordinary conversation, requests are often put in the form of a question. Similarly, reported requests often look like reported questions.

He asked me if I could lend him £5.

Unit 18

could have done

1 You use *could*, *may* or *might* with *have* to say that it is possible that something was the case, but you don't know if it was the case or not.

64

GRAMMAR REFERENCE

The barman *could/may/might have killed* Celia Mallinson. = It is possible that he killed her, but you don't know for sure.

2 You also use *could* with *have* to show that there was a possibility of something happening in the past, although it did not happen.
   He *could have got* a job last year. = It was possible, but he didn't do it.

3 You use *could not have* to say that it is impossible that something happened or was the case.
   They *couldn't have been* there at 7.00 am. = It is impossible that they were there.
   You use *may/might not have* to say that it is possible that something did not happen or was not the case.
   They *might not have been* there at 7.00 am. = It is possible that they were not there.

Unit 19

has been done

1 The present perfect passive is formed by using the present perfect of *be* and the past participle of the main verb.
   Real progress *has been made* - a new airport *has been built*.

2 The present perfect tense in the passive can be used with adjuncts like *just*, *already*, and *yet*.
   A new airstrip *has just been built*.
   The entire city *has not been excavated yet*.

3 See Unit 9 Grammar Reference for the uses of the passive.

Unit 20

indefinite article: *a, an*

1 *A* and *an* are the commonest general determiners. They are used to talk about people or things in an indefinite way. You put *a* or *an* in front of the singular form of a countable noun when you are mentioning that noun for the first time.
   He was eating *an apple*.
   He picked up *a book*.

2 You use *a* a) in front of a consonant. *A good book*. b) before words that begin with a vowel, but whose first sound is y. *A university*.

3 You use *an* when the word begins with a vowel sound.
   an open book   *an hour*

4 You can use *a(n)* in a noun group after some verbs like *be, become, feel, look, seem, sound, make,* to give more information about someone or something.
   She *is a model*.
   His brother *was a sensitive child*.

5 You can use *a(n)* with a noun when you are using one example to make a general statement about all people or things of that type.
   A dog likes to eat more meat than *a human being*.

definite article: *the*

1 You can use *the* with any noun if it is obvious who or what you are referring to from what has already been said or written.

2 There are many situations where you have to add something to the noun to make it clear who or what you are referring to:
   a) the + *adjective* + noun - the *large, white* building.
   b) the + noun + *prepositional phrase* - ... the girl *in the car*.
   c) the + noun + *relative clause* - ... the woman *who left late*.
   d) the + noun + *to + infinitive* - the thing *to aim* for ...

3 *The* is also used:
   a) when there is just one person, place or thing in a particular place.
      There's a wind coming off *the river*.
   b) with countable nouns which are used in the singular to refer to something more general.
      They broke *the law*. = the system of laws in a country.
   c) with nouns referring to living things when you are making a statement about every member of a species.
      Australia is the home of *the kangaroo*.

zero article

1 You can sometimes use a noun without a determiner when you are referring to people or things in an indefinite way.
   We are raising money for *charity*.
   Visitors must not walk on the grass.

2 Uncountable nouns are usually used without a determiner.
   He had *wealth* and *power*.
   The donkey needed *food* and *water*.

3 Plural nouns are used without a determiner when you are referring to all people or things of a particular kind.
   Are there any jobs that *men* can do that *women* can't?

4 Plural nouns can also be used without a determiner to refer to an unspecified number of things.
   Parents should read *stories* to children.

Tapescripts

Unit 1
Exercise 4: Personal space

Part 1

I Dr Crewe, you've been studying non-verbal communication, or body language, for some time now. First of all, can you explain what body language is?

Dr C Yes. Body language refers to the ways that people communicate non-verbally, or without words, using means like gesture, facial expression or even tone of voice. It also refers to things like the way people feel about territories and their own personal space.

I Personal space? What's that?

Dr C That's the area of space around you that you claim as your own - like a personal air bubble that each person carries around with him or her. If other people, particularly strangers, enter that space, then you begin to feel very uncomfortable.

I Is each person's personal space the same then?

Dr C Oh no. In fact, personal space differs from culture to culture. In smaller countries, like Japan, the space is relatively small, about 25 cm, but in less crowded countries, like America, the space is much larger - it's about 46 cm.

I I see.

Part 2

I In your experience, are people aware of body language?

Dr C Well, er, people like actors, salesmen, politicians, have been reading and using body language for some time. But it's a language that most ordinary people are not aware of. People don't realise it, but only 7% of a message comes from the actual words we use. The rest, that's 93% of a message, comes from our tone of voice and body language.

I Really? That's amazing! So if people don't understand body language, can this lead to misunderstandings?

Dr C Oh yes. Let me give you an example. I mentioned personal space?

I Yes.

Dr C Well, as I suggested, people with a smaller personal space, like the Japanese, will stand or sit much closer to one another than people with a larger personal space, like an American.

I Um-hum.

Dr C Well, I er, attended a conference recently in America and I noticed that when a Japanese was speaking to an American, the two actually began to move around the room. The American was moving backwards and the Japanese gradually moving towards him.

I Really? Why was that?

Dr C Well, because when the Japanese businessman, with his smaller personal space, moved forward, he entered the American's larger personal space. This made the American uncomfortable, so he moved back. The Japanese in turn moved forward, the American moved back, and so on. In fact, video recordings played at high speed give the impression that both men are dancing around the conference room, with the Japanese leading.

I So can this lead to misunderstandings?

Dr C Well, of course. In the example I just gave you, it could lead to the Japanese businessman thinking that the American was cold and unfriendly, because he kept moving away from him. On the other hand, the American could think that the Japanese businessman was too aggressive. Not understanding another culture's body language can lead to all sorts of misunderstandings.

Exercise 7

Dialogue A

M Have you seen the new Brock Hanson film? It's really good.
W Really?

Dialogue B

M I've just picked up the photographs of my holiday in Blackpool.
W Really?

Dialogue C

W1 How does it look?
W2 I've told you, it looks great.
W1 Really?

Unit 2
Exercise 2: ActionAid

I ActionAid was founded in 1972 by the late Cecil Jackson Cole. It operates programmes in Africa, Asia and Latin America and is now one of Britain's leading overseas development agencies. With us this morning we have a spokeswoman for ActionAid. Could you tell us who ActionAid helps?

S Well, ActionAid is working to improve conditions for children in poor countries. But we believe that we can make real, and lasting improvements only if we help families and indeed whole villages to overcome poverty.

I I see. So you aim to help children in poor countries by helping their families and the villages where they live as well.

S Yes. We work directly with the whole community to develop long-term programmes that will help them to overcome their poverty.

I What sort of long-term programmes?

S Well, in some areas we have set up schools for children. We also help people to improve the way that they farm, er, we show them how to protect their environment, how to improve their health care and fight disease, and many other things.

TAPESCRIPTS

I Mhmm, so how can people help these children and their communities through ActionAid?

S Well, there are basically two ways people can help. One is by sponsoring a child. To sponsor a child you must give a sum of money every month. That money goes to help a child, its family and the community. The other way people can help is by giving money to one of our development projects overseas. Either way, you can give direct help to children, families and to entire communities that are in need.

I Thank you very much. Now, next on our programme we have ...

Exercise 6: Ages of responsibility

I What are your rights and responsibilities as a child or teenager in Britain?

X Well, as young as the age of ten, you can be convicted of a criminal offence, though it must be proved that you knew what you were doing at the time of the crime. If you are held by the police, you will be old enough to be searched, fingerprinted and photographed. On the other hand, erm, you can't buy a pet until you are 12 years old. When you are 13, you can work part-time, but you can't work for more than two hours on a school day or on a Sunday. You can go into a pub at the age of 14, but you can't buy or drink alcohol there. With your parents' consent, you can leave home or marry when you are 16. At 16 you can also leave school, apply for your own passport, and drink beer, wine or cider with a meal in a restaurant. And, when you are 17, you can drive most vehicles, including a plane. You can also be used by another person to beg in the street. And finally, at the age of 18 you legally become an adult: you can vote, serve on a jury, change your name, make your will - and you can even donate your body to science if you wish.

Unit 3

Exercise 2: Listening to literature

Part 1

I So, Mike, you're a teacher at a College of Further Education, and you, er, you teach English literature.

M That's right. I've taught here at this college for seven years.

I One thing that students ask, when they hear about you, is how is it possible that a person who's blind can teach English literature? I mean, it's to do with reading books, and they don't quite understand. Can you explain how it works?

M Yes, in terms of my own ability to read the books, there are two methods that I would use for that - either listening to the books on tape or reading them in Braille. Both the tape books and the Braille books come from two national libraries that have many, many thousands of books in them, so I can usually get hold of a book or else it can be added to the library. The other thing that people sometimes ask me is how I mark the students' work.

I Mhmm, mhmm.

M And for that I use readers, people who read to me, read the essays, er, and put down the comments. They have the red pen, and they will write down my comments. And after a while I become quite quick at doing that.

I Is it always the same person, like a friend?

M Oh, no. They're people that I pay, or rather, the government gives me money to pay for them.

I Mhmm.

Part 2

I Do you ever get a strange reaction from students?

M I think that erm, they're curious, and perhaps even a little afraid at first, because they're wondering what it's going to be like. I think particularly in the first two or three lessons, students are very unsure, but I think after a while they stop thinking about that - they don't think about me so much as a teacher who can't see, but as Mike, who has a number of peculiarities, one of which is that he can't see.

I And would you say that the fact that they see someone who's blind doing this job perfectly competently has an effect on them over and above what they learn about English?

M Oh yes, I'm sure. I think it's very good for the students, and for the College to employ people with disabilities. I think that uhm, on the whole in our society, disabled people and people who are able-bodied don't have much contact with one another - in fact the majority of disabled people, more than 60%, don't get jobs, and because of this, disabled and able-bodied people don't get to know each other. And that makes things worse, because as long as people, don't think about disability, then society continues to be very badly designed for disabled people and so the whole thing goes on and on.

Exercise 6: I think it's a ...

(Sound effects)

Unit 4

Exercise 3: Radio news

Part 1

Here are tonight's news headlines. Kidnapped millionaire John Croft has been allowed to go free. Customs agents in America have discovered a 100-foot tunnel beneath the US border with Mexico. In Essex, three people have died in a fire in their home, and a lonely clerk has left nearly half a million pounds to an animal charity.

Part 2

Now, here is the news in detail. Millionaire John Croft was freed yesterday when his kidnappers were paid the £100,000 that they were asking for his release. However, within hours of Mr Croft's release, police had arrested five men and had recovered most of the money. Mr Croft, who was kidnapped five days ago, is presently resting with his family. American customs officers have discovered a 100-foot drug tunnel beneath the US border with Mexico which has been used for smuggling cocaine into the country. Officers think that the tunnel was in use for 6 months before it was discovered, and that up to five tons of cocaine were hidden in the tunnel. The investigation continues. A man, woman and their nine-year-old child died last night when their house burnt to the ground. The police say that all three people

TAPESCRIPTS

probably died in their sleep from breathing in smoke and poisonous gases. The cause of the fire is not yet known. A clerk, John Bailey, has died and left £469,887 to an animal charity. Mr Bailey's only relative, his uncle Fred Stott, received next to nothing. Neighbours of Mr Bailey were stunned to hear of his fortune. He had a Labrador dog, but was not a member of the animal charity.

Part 3
And finally an 18-year-old schoolgirl has won half a million pounds in a major lottery. Miss Lee received her cheque at her school where she was busy with her final exams.

Unit 5

Exercise 5: Youth awards
... and that's it for the news at 9.00. Now as you all know in a few days we're going to be announcing the winners of the Best of British Youth Awards 1990, held by Radio 4, and the YMCA, and sponsored by the National Westminster Bank. In case you haven't heard, the 6 finalists this year are: first of all Lorraine Brackley, aged 18. Lorraine spends most of her free time caring for patients in the geriatric unit of her local hospital. She arrives at the hospital at 7.45 am every day and spends 2 hours there before going to College. She has also started a scheme to make sure that elderly patients receive cards and presents on special occasions. Lorraine often keeps in touch with patients who have no family after they leave the hospital. The second finalist is Michael Cude, aged 17 from the Rhondda Valley in Wales. Michael has set up Youth Link Rhondda, which is managed by young people to help educate other young people about drug and alcohol abuse, a major problem in the area. The group has recently set up a very popular no-alcohol bar at a local youth club which attracts up to 150 teenagers every Friday night. Kerry Noble, aged 16, has cerebral palsy. At 14, she successfully campaigned for automatic doors to be installed at her local supermarket. These doors made it possible for people in wheelchairs to get in and out of the supermarket. Kerry has also been involved in promoting 'Seawell', a centre which helps disabled young people get out and appreciate the countryside. Recently, she has set up a project called 'Hope', which aims to give disabled people the opportunity to take part in sporting events alongside able-bodied people. Louis O'Leary, the fourth finalist, is 17. At school he was labelled 'disruptive and rebellious'. He was expelled from school, without any qualifications, and for some time he drifted from job to job. But in 1989 he met a group of mentally disabled young people on the beach and shortly after that he became a volunteer worker at their local school. He now works for the school full-time, looking after people with severe behavioural problems. Louis loves his job and is a highly valued member of the staff team. Alex Saddington, aged 21, has spent much of his life in care. At the age of 16, he left school without any qualifications. But he has managed to overcome his past experiences and now spends his time helping other children and young people in care. He has founded 'Kent in Care', an organisation campaigning for the rights of children in care. Finally, Amanda Turner, aged 21, is suffering from a rare form of terminal cancer. Amanda is in constant pain, but nevertheless she aims to raise one million pounds for medical equipment for her local hospital. Although it cannot help Mandy, the equipment will help to save the lives of many others. Amanda attends many fund-raising events in her community, and so far she has helped raise £650,000. Six deserving young people.

Unit 6

Exercise 6: It has its ups and downs

Part 1
I Why did you choose to live on a houseboat?
B The reasons were mainly financial, because an average house in those days cost about £5,000 and a houseboat of any size was about £2,000, so it was really quite a lot cheaper to buy the houseboat.
I Mhmm. Once you had the boat, were you allowed to take it wherever you liked?
B Well, there were restrictions on where you could moor the boats, depending on the length of time that you wanted to be there. But we couldn't move ours because it didn't have an engine. It wasn't mobile, and most of the houseboats alongside us were not moveable either. But there are definite restrictions on where you can live in houseboats because the houseboats themselves have to be connected to water and electricity.
I I see. Was it a very large boat?
B Well, we looked at several, and, erm, it was a motor torpedo boat that was built in 1945, just towards the end of the war. It was 120 feet long and 24 feet wide. So, yes, it was a large boat.

Part 2
I I see. It's an unusual lifestyle. Were there any particular advantages to it, do you think?
B Yes, definitely. Especially for younger people, and we were younger then. It was a very carefree life and a very friendly one. If you liked country living, it was absolutely ideal, and we were right in the middle of the country, and the river and the yachts were very, very beautiful. And there was a tremendous sense of freedom, and wonderful for the children - they enjoyed it and they didn't know of the hardships.
I Were there many hardships?
B Oh yes, there were a great deal. It may sound strange, but we had no privacy. There were no bells, you see, and anybody could just walk on and off your home. And it was difficult to get anything onto the boat, because it all had to go up the gangplanks, which were only 3 feet wide. In the winter we were very, very cold and damp all the time, because of the leaks. And of course, the gales hit one extremely hard. It's a very, very physically hard life.

Part 3
B It's a very, very physically hard life.
I Yes, it sounds it. Are there any incidents that you particularly remember?

TAPESCRIPTS

B Yes, when we first bought the boat and went to live on it, it was August and for 3 weeks of that month we had very hot, dry weather. We were totally green and we had no experience in maintaining a houseboat and nobody told us - they seemed to let you learn the hard way. When it rained for the first time, it rained after 3 weeks of dry weather, and the rain just poured right through the deck - we were just sitting there in the rain in our home. Nobody had told us that you had to put roofing felt on the deck to stop the rain coming in. So the next day we had to go out and buy roofing felt for the entire boat - so leaks were always a problem - always. Nobody was leak-proof.

I Goodness! On balance, though, was it a good experience do you think?

B Oh yes, it had its ups and downs, of course, but on balance, it was a very good experience. There were a tremendous number of laughs. Everybody had the same sort of experiences, and they were very carefree. It was an experience I wouldn't have done without now, but I would say you need to be young and healthy to enjoy it.

Unit 7
Exercise 3: Radio advice

Reply 1
Oh, dear! You're being asked to choose between your husband and your children and that is a very difficult situation. Your husband thinks he has the right to tell you what to do, but no one has that right - it's your life! I can understand him feeling that your children might take you away from him when he obviously loves you very much, but you must talk to him. Why don't you explain that you love him and that you have no intention of leaving him, but that you would love to be able to share your children with him. In the end, you must do what you want - not what your husband thinks you ought to do.

Reply 2
Well, that depends on what you want from your boyfriend. After 3 years you must be happy together and he must be content with his life, otherwise he would have found a job. You must ask yourself what you're looking for in a boyfriend and if you realise that he's right for you, accept him the way he is. Of course, when you decide to marry, he will need to face up to the realities of clothing, feeding and housing a family. That's something he can't ignore, especially if you're the only one earning a wage.

Reply 3
I think you might be surprised! If she is often where you are and talks to you, then it looks to me like she's already noticed you. A few months isn't a very long time, and she will respect you more for not being pushy and over-confident. As you are usually outgoing, perhaps this girl is suddenly making you realise that sometimes you have to be a bit quieter and more considerate in life. Just talk to her alone one evening and tell her how much you like her, then just see what happens!

Unit 8
Exercise 3: Colour in your life

I Miss Fox, you work as a colour consultant. Can you explain what what means?

JF Yes, of course. Well, first of all, I believe that the colours that we wear and have around us have a powerful effect on the way we feel, and on the way other people react to us. So, I try to make people aware of the effects of colour on themselves and on the people around them.

I I see.

JF Yes, so, for example, I advise people on which colours they should have around themselves in their homes, and I also advise them on which colours they should wear, both to make themselves feel better, and to create the right impression for other people.

I Can you give us an example?

JF Yes, of course. Red, for example. Red is a very energetic colour, and wearing red can make you seem as if you have a lot of energy and are very independent. On the other hand, wearing too much red can create the impression that you're an angry, aggressive sort of person, so you have to be careful not to overdo it.

I Well, I'll take your advice and throw out my red tracksuit then!

JF Oh no, don't do that. Red will give you energy - you need energy if you're running or exercising.

I Oh, good! So what can you say about some of the other colours. Can you give us any advice about them?

JF Uhm..orange. Orange is a cheerful colour, and people who wear orange seem cheerful, of course, and they also appear to be interested in other people. A nice sunny yellow is a colour that many people like. Yellow is the colour of charm, and optimism and pure joy. I find that people who have a lot of self-confidence often wear yellow.

I As it happens, I'm wearing green today. What does that say about me?

JF Green. Of course, we're hearing a lot about green these days with all the talk about the environment.

I Yes . . .

JF But green also represents balance, and tradition - things that stay the same.

I I'm not sure if that's good news, or not. What about blue?

JF Well, blue is a very calm, peaceful colour - people who wear blue can look as if they're able to cope with anything. On the other hand, blue can be a sad, depressing colour if you wear too much of it, so you have to be careful.

I Well, this all sounds like good advice. Now, you said earlier that you also advise people on the best colours to paint the rooms in their house.

JF Yes, that's right. Well, I wouldn't for example, advise anyone to paint their bedroom bright red, at least not if they want to get any sleep...

TAPESCRIPTS
Unit 9
Exercise 2: Holiday upset

N Anne! You're back! How was your holiday?
A Terrible!
N Oh no! What went wrong?
A What didn't go wrong? That'd be a better question. You know we left on Friday night with our so-called experienced coach driver? Well, he couldn't even find his way to Dover! He set off north instead of south and Jack had to direct him. Anyway, we finally got on the ferry, and that was OK, until we got on the mainland and back on the coach.
N And then what happened?
A The coach broke down! It hadn't been checked properly before we set off, I guess. It was hours before we got underway again. Anyway, at long last we got going, and then we discovered that there was no food or drink on the coach - they'd put it all on the wrong coach, would you believe?
N Oh no! So what happened next?
A Well, nothing for a while. And then the coach driver got lost again - he couldn't find the right resort and once again Jack had to direct him. Can you believe it? Anyway, we got there at last, thanks to Jack.
N And how was your room? Was that all right?
A No, it was not! It was filthy - it looked as though it hadn't been cleaned properly in months. Of course, I complained to the representatives, but it wasn't cleaned even then, so I had to do it myself. That took me a whole day and at the end of it I thought, at last, I can sit down and relax, and I discovered that I couldn't close the curtains - so we had no privacy either!
N Oh, dear!
A On the following day, we took the children down to the pool and we discovered that the large pool hadn't even been filled and the children's pool that they'd promised us in the brochure didn't exist. Oh, and neither did the poolside bar we'd been promised.
N So what did you do then?
A We went back to the room to talk it over only to find that the representatives, who had the apartment above ours, were playing such loud music we had to get away! I tell you, it was the worst holiday I've ever had. I'm glad to be home.
N So what are you going to do about it?
A Well, I've got a complaints form to fill out. But you know, I'm so angry, I think I'm going to ask for our money back.
N I should think so! It sounds as if you deserve it.

Exercise 5: Consumer rights
Dialogue A

S Good afternoon. Can I help you?
C Are you the manager?
S Yes, I am.
C Well, I'm afraid I have a complaint to make. I bought this watch from your shop a week ago, and it's stopped working. I'd like to exchange it for another one.
S Do you have a receipt?
C Here.
S Yes, well. I'm afraid it's not our policy to replace items. The best that we can do is send the watch back to the manufacturer's and ask them to repair it.
C And how long will that take?
S About three to four weeks.

Dialogue B

S Good morning. Do you need any help?
C Yes, I do. I'd like to return this coat.
S Oh? Is it damaged?
C No, it's not damaged. I came in here yesterday, not really looking for anything in particular, and I saw this coat. I wasn't sure it suited me, but the sales assistant was very persuasive and in the end I decided to take the coat. But I've changed my mind - it really doesn't suit me at all, and I'd like my money back.
S Ah, I'm afraid it's not our policy to give refunds unless the item is damaged in some way. The best we can do is offer you a credit note.
C But I wouldn't have bought the coat in the first place if your assistant hadn't talked me into it!

Dialogue C

I Good morning, ladies and gentlemen. And in our studio this morning we have Clare Morgan, a consumer affairs specialist, to give you some advice on your rights as consumers. We already have some callers, so let's get started! Good morning.
C1 Good morning. I'm calling about a problem I have with a jeweller's. About two weeks ago I bought a watch and unfortunately one week later it had stopped working. So I took the watch back to the jeweller's where I'd bought it and asked them to exchange it, which they refused to do. What's worse, they said that I would have to wait 3-4 weeks while they sent the watch away to be repaired. As I'd only had the watch a week, that hardly seems fair. But can I demand my money back?
CM Unfortunately, your problem isn't a straightforward one. Legally, your complaint is with the person who sold you the watch and on those grounds you could insist on a refund. However, the problem is that the seller could say that the watch was in good working order when he sold it to you, and that you've damaged it in some way. I know it's frustrating, but in your position, I think I'd let them send the watch away to be repaired. I'm sorry I can't give you more encouraging advice.
C1 Well, thanks very much for your help anyway.
I Caller number 2.
C2 Good morning. Erm, about a week ago, I bought a very expensive coat from a shop. The thing is, I really wasn't sure about the coat at the time, but the sales assistant was very persuasive, and she talked me into it. Well, when I got the coat home, I realised I'd made a terrible mistake. It looked dreadful on me. So I took it back the next day, but they told me I couldn't have my money back - I'd have to accept a credit note instead. Well, I mean, as I didn't want the coat in the first

TAPESCRIPTS

place, I wasn't exactly satisfied with that. Can I take the coat back and demand a refund?
CM I'm afraid not. Unfortunately, you don't have any rights to return an item you've bought simply because you decide you don't like it. To keep good customer relations some shops will give a refund or, as in your case, a credit note. But they're not even obliged to do that. I'm very sorry
C2 Oh, well. Thanks very much anyway.
I Next caller, please!

Unit 10
Exercise 2: Point of difference
I Are you ready?
Bob Sure, why not.
I Ok, question number 1. If you heard a cat meowing faintly, how easily could you place the cat without looking round?
Bob Uhmm, I'm not sure. I'm sure I could point to the cat ... if I thought about it a little.
I Right. Now, how good would you say you are at remembering a song you've just heard? Could you sing it, do you think?
Bob Sing it? No, never. I've got no ear for music at all, I'm afraid.
I None at all?
Bob No, I'm afraid not.
I Now imagine then that a person you've met only a few times rings you up. In the first few seconds of the conversation, could you easily tell whose voice it was?
Bob Mhmm, it depends. I'd certainly recognise the voice some of the time.
I Yeah? How often? Half the time? Less than half? More than half?
Bob Mhmm, more than half, I suppose.
I More than half. Ok. In your early schooldays, how easy did you find spelling and the writing of essays?
Bob Well, my spelling was never that great. But I was pretty good at writing essays.
I Ok. Do you drive?
Bob Of course.
I Ok, so imagine you've found a place to park your car, but it's a small space and to make matters worse, you have to back into it. What would you do?
Bob Well, I'd back into it, of course. What else could I do?
I I don't know. Now, imagine you're in a strange village and you've been there for three days. If someone asked you which way was north, do you think you could tell them?
Bob I'm sure I could tell them. I've got a very good sense of direction.
I Have you?
Bob Yes.
I Right, last question now. You're in a dentist's waiting room with several people of the same sex. How close could you sit to one of them without feeling uncomfortable? Fifteen centimetres, 15-60 centimetres, or over 60 centimetres?
Bob Oh well, I know that sitting very close to someone makes me feel very uncomfortable. I'd have to say over 60 centimetres.
I Over 60 centimetres. Now let me add up your score... Mhm, I know you'll be happy to hear that according to the quiz, your brain is definitely more male than female.
Bob Well, I could have told you that in the first place!

Unit 11
Exercise 5: A festival
I Chi, when does Chinese New Year take place?
C That depends. Sometimes it comes in January and sometimes it starts in February, the beginning of February. It takes place at the first full moon.
I Why do people celebrate Chinese New Year?
C They celebrate Chinese New Year because that will bring good fortune to them for the next year, and also to give thanks for the harvest they grew last year and the profit they made last year.
I And they hope it will bring profit for the year to come, for the new year?
C Yes.
I What do people do to prepare for the celebrations at Chinese New Year?
C The first thing they do is save up money and buy new stuff for the new year. We also clean our houses, and pay our debts from the year before. And we decorate our houses - we use red in a lot of the decorations because it is the luckiest colour. And also we prepare some special food as well for the New Year. On Hong Kong island they also have beautiful all-night flower markets and thousands of people go there to buy their flowers for the New Year's day.
I And on the New Year day, do you arrange family gatherings?
C Mainly we go to visit our friends and family who are out of reach during the year because they're working. And we will also go to pray as well, because most of the people in Hong Kong believe in the Buddhist religion.
I Mhmm, mhmm. Chi, at Chinese New Year, when the celebrations take place, what do people wear and what special things do they eat? And what other things do they do to actually celebrate the New Year?
C First they will wear new clothes if they can. And they eat special sweets after dinner, which they prepare. They're supposed to eat these sweets because they will bring good luck and prosperity. And also, they will go to a Buddhist temple.
I What about processions and firework displays and things like that?
C They don't have many on Hong Kong island, but on the outer islands on Macau or the new territory they have firework displays and also the lion dance.
I It all sounds quite spectacular.
C Yes, yes it can be.

TAPESCRIPTS

Unit 12
Exercise 5: Space travel

I When America was putting men on the moon in the 1960s, nobody questioned the US space programme. But in more recent years, people's attitudes have begun to change. America, Russia and many other countries have spent billions of pounds on space exploration and this year the budget for the US space programme alone is seven billion dollars. Dr Green, don't you think that space exploration is simply too expensive and that the money could be better spent right here on earth?

Dr Well, let me first answer that by saying that if you look at the amounts of money that governments spend, seven billion dollars isn't really that much money. I mean, do you realise that one space rocket costs less than a nuclear submarine?

I No, I have to say I didn't know that. But nevertheless, some people would still say: why spend any money at all on space programmes when we have so many important problems right here on earth that we really need to solve? Seven billion dollars after all would feed a lot of hungry people.

Dr Yes, of course that's true. On the other hand, space exploration could help feed some of those hungry people, believe it or not.

I How's that?

Dr Well, very soon we're going to have too many people on earth and too few resources to support them. That's part of the reason why people are starving right now. But space exploration could change all that.

I How?

Dr By giving mankind the opportunity to spread out and move away from earth. Right now there are plans for building giant space colonies where thousands of people would live and grow their own food. Eventually, whole industries may be moved from earth and housed in the space colonies. What's more, by the beginning of the next century, the first colonies on the moon should have been started. And eventually a lot of our metals and even electricity could come from space and other planets. I Anything else?

Dr Oh, yes, lots. The human race is going to enter a new age of travelling and living in space. Space shuttles will make travelling in space as common as aeroplane flights are today. Future wars may even be fought in space.

I Well, that's certainly something to look forward to. But even if what you say is true, none of that is going to happen for many years. Have we gained anything from the space programme that's of any real use today?

Dr Well, we've gained a lot of knowledge, of course, though some people wouldn't place much value on that. But there are also many things that you use in your day-to-day life that we wouldn't have without the space programme - satellite television, microwave ovens, even cake mixes.

I Oh, well, we couldn't live without those, could we? Now, what about safety?...

Unit 13
Exercise 2: How to succeed

Dialogue A

D I think the most important thing you must have to succeed in Italy is er . . . of course, you have to be ambitious, because if you are not ambitious you can't reach your aim, your target. And you must have also a natural ability, because you must adapt yourself and your work and er enjoy your work, of course. And Italian people are used to working a lot and to doing hard work. Of course you must also know the right people because if you want a job and you don't know anybody you have to work much harder.

I So if you were going to choose one factor, Dario, which one do you think would be the most important? Could you choose one?

D Yes, ambition.

I Ambition. Thank you.

Dialogue B

S I think that to be successful in Spain you need ambition, because it's what makes you want to work and to do something different. And I think natural ability is also important. To be a good musician and to succeed I think that you must have something special. And I think that knowing the right people is important because it can save you a lot of time. You don't spend so much time trying to get something if you know people that can help you.

I What would you say is the most important thing?

S Ambition I think is the most important.

Dialogue C

T I think the most important things are hard work, and good education, and natural ability. The Japanese have a traditional culture and we think that working in-
dustriously is a virtue, so laziness cannot be accepted by society. And a good education - anyone who wants to and who makes the effort can enter the famous universities, so er, when we estimate someone's ability we look at whether he's graduated from university or not. But if someone wants to succeed, of course he need ambition and natural ability.

I So for you, which is the most important factor?

T Oh, in Japan, hard work, definitely.

Unit 14
Exercise 2: A good night's sleep

We spend almost one third of our lives asleep, and by the time we are seventy-five years old, we have slept for at least twenty-five years, and have been dreaming for about ten of those years. We experience dreams four or five times each night for periods of a few seconds to half an hour. Studies have shown that dreams decrease with age: newly-born babies dream for 80% of their total sleeping time; children dream 35-40% of their total sleeping time, and adults 20-30%. Animals also dream, though some more than others. Scientists think they have discovered that fish never dream, and that birds dream very little. Reptiles,

TAPESCRIPTS

tortoises and snakes never dream, though they spend 60% of their time asleep. All mammals dream, but they are divided into two groups, the hunters and the hunted. The hunters, like cats and dogs, dream 20-25% of their sleep time, while the hunted, like rabbits and sheep, dream only 8% of their sleep-time. There is much disagreement about the meaning and purpose of dreams, but one thing is certain - man, and indeed animals, cannot survive without them. In experiments with people who have been prevented from dreaming, the people became so disturbed that the experimenters had to stop the tests. And in similar experiments with animals, cats and rats in otherwise perfect health have died.

Exercise 6: A dream come true?

A I had this particular dream a few years ago. I'd received a very nice watch for my twenty-first birthday, so of course it had sentimental value as well as real value. And then that spring, I went to Germany to study for a term. I'd completed an insurance form before I left, and on the form I'd mentioned the watch specifically as an item of particular value. Anyhow, I went swimming one afternoon, and I left the watch on a hanger when I went into the pool, but when I returned the watch had gone.

B Oh no!

A Yeah. Anyhow, I made the insurance claim and returned to England, where I immediately started looking for a watch to replace the one I'd lost. In the end, I'd gone all round the London jewellers, and looked at all the watchmaker's catalogues, and I still couldn't find a watch like mine. I was so disappointed.

B I can imagine.

A And then I had this dream - I dreamt that I saw a watch - my watch - in a jeweller's window. And would you believe it, the very next day, I went to a local shopping centre - I was feeling very unhappy because I hadn't been able to find my watch - and I looked in a jeweller's window, and there it was - my watch. Isn't that amazing?

B Incredible!

Unit 15

Exercise 2: No regrets

Part 1

I Helen, you were going to be a gymnastics teacher, weren't you?

H Yes. I did think about it, but it was going to be too expensive.

I You mean the training?

H The training, yes.

I So you went to secretarial college.

H I did.

I Mhmm

H And I have no regrets.

I Really, you enjoyed it?

H Oh, I did, very much.

I Didn't you feel sad that you couldn't become a teacher?

H Well, in a way, but as time went on I had no regrets.

I Really? ...

Part 2

I Where did you train, Glasgow, wasn't it, to be a secretary?

H Yes, Glasgow.

I That was a long way from home.

H Yes, I had two hours to travel morning and evening to get back home.

I Really. And did you manage to continue with your sports at all?

H No, I didn't because by the time I got home at night it would have been too late to do any training and I had my homework to do. And in any case there were no proper training facilities in the country where I lived.

I When you say none do you mean none at all?

H None at all. I did my training in a field where horses and cows grazed.

I Goodness. Everybody expects sports tracks and things these days, don't they?

H Yes, but not in those days. That was over 50 years ago, you know.

I Gosh, I suppose it was. But would it have made a difference if you had lived in the city?

H Oh yes, if I'd lived in a city I would have had many opportunities to join a club for instance where they had proper training facilities. But living in the country, it would have taken me a long time to get to the nearest city to do any training, and it wouldn't have been worthwhile.

I I suppose the nearest city was Glasgow, two hours away.

H That's right, yes.

I And you had to come home every night after college?

H That's right.

I And don't you ever wish that you'd been able to become a gym teacher, now?

H It would have been a nice prospect, but, uh, I think I enjoyed my secretarial years so much that I have no regrets.

Exercise 6: The Silent Couple

Once upon a time there was a newly-married couple. They were still dressed in their wedding clothes and relaxing in their new home after the last of the guests had left. 'Dear husband' said the wife, 'do go and close the door. It is open onto the street.' 'Me shut it?' said the groom. 'A bridegroom in his splendid clothes with priceless robe and a dagger studded with jewels? You must be out of your mind - go and shut it yourself!' 'So!' shouted the bride. 'You expect me to be your slave: a gentle, beautiful creature like me, wearing a dress of finest silk - that I should get up on my wedding day and close a door? Impossible!' They were both silent for a minute, and then the bride suggested a way to solve the problem. Whoever spoke first would get up and close the door. There were two sofas in the room and the couple settled themselves, one on each sofa, face to face, saying nothing. They had been like this for some time when a party of thieves came by and noticed that the door was open. The robbers crept into the silent house and began to rob it of everything that they could lay their hands on. The husband and

TAPESCRIPTS

wife heard the robbers, but each thought that the other should attend to the matter, and neither of them spoke. Mistaking the man and his wife for wax dummies, the robbers even stripped them of their personal jewels, and still the couple said nothing. The thieves made off with everything that the couple possessed, and the bride and groom sat on their sofas throughout the night, saying nothing. When daylight came, a policeman saw the open door and walked into the house. He asked the couple what had happened and, of course, neither of them would reply. The officer at last lost his temper and said to the husband, 'I will give you a blow, and perhaps then you will speak to me!' At this, the wife could not restrain herself: 'Please,' she begged, 'do not hit him - he is my husband!'

The end
The officer at last lost his temper and said to the husband, 'I will give you a blow, and perhaps then you will speak to me!' At this, the wife could not restrain herself: 'Please,' she begged, 'do not hit him - he is my husband!' 'I won,' shouted the husband immediately, 'so you have to shut the door!'

Unit 16
Exercise 3: Global warming

I On our programme this afternoon we're going to be talking about a subject that has been getting a lot of attention recently - and that is global warming. For years now, some scientists have been warning us about global warming. But just how serious is the problem and what can we do to prevent the situation from getting worse? With us this morning, we have Dr Stokes from the weather office. First of all, Dr Stokes, what causes global warming?

Dr Well, basically global warming is caused by an increase in the amount of carbon dioxide in the atmosphere. Carbon dioxide is rather like a giant blanket around the earth, and it keeps the heat in the atmosphere. If the amount of CO_2 in the air doubled, for example, the earth's temperature would rise by about 2 degrees centigrade, or 4 degrees Fahrenheit.

I That doesn't sound like much.

Dr No, it doesn't. But it would be enough to melt the polar ice caps. This would raise sea levels by about 60 metres or 200 feet, which in turn would be enough to drown coastal cities like New York, Bombay and London.

I I see. That is frightening. Well, it is true to say that we've already started to see changes in the world's weather.

Dr Oh, yes. The droughts in Africa, for example. And unless we act now, more and more people will starve because their croplands have become deserts.

I What do you mean by 'unless we act now'? What can we do?

Dr Well, first of all, let me say that even if we start to make changes now, we may not be able to reverse all the damage. For example, I think that the weather in some parts of the world has been changed forever. But unless we can reduce the amount of carbon dioxide going into the atmosphere, we're going to have even more serious problems.

I And how can we do that?

Dr Well, to begin with, we have to...

Unit 17
Exercise 3: Doctor's orders

Dr Come in
P Good morning, doctor
Dr Good morning, Mr. Duncan. Now, what's the problem?
P Well, I've got this terrible pain in my stomach and feel like I'm going to be sick.
Dr Can you describe this pain?
P It started in the middle, but now it's here the whole time, on the right.
Dr OK. Just lie down here, that's it. Now, er, how long have you had this pain?
P It started yesterday, but it's been getting worse all day.
Dr Are you eating much?
P Oh, I haven't really eaten anything since yesterday. I don't have much of an appetite.
Dr Do you feel feverish?
P Well, I do feel a bit hot.
Dr Ok, pull up your shirt and show me where it hurts the most.
P It's here.
Dr I'll be very gentle and feel your tummy. But just tell me if it hurts.
P Ohhh, ohhh, arrrr, arr.
Dr That's where it's most painful is it?
P Oh, yes.
Dr Well, I think you may have appendicitis, which could mean an operation. Now, you lie here whilst I arrange your admission and transport to hospital.

Exercise 6: Roleplay

Dialogue A

Dr Hello, Mr Campbell. And what seems to be the problem?
MC I keep getting these terrible headaches.
Dr How often are you getting them?
MC Oh, I don't know. About er, once a week. But when one comes it generally lasts all day.
Dr Have you noticed anything else that happens when you have these headaches?
MC Yes. I feel sick, and sometimes I vomit.
Dr Do you have any problem with your vision?
MC Well, I don't like the light on, it seems to flash and make me feel even worse.
Dr Mhmm, does anything make you feel better?
MC Not really. I just have to lie down in a dark room.
Dr Right, well, they sound like migraine headaches, and in some people certain foods like chocolate or cheese can actually trigger them off. Perhaps you could take note if they seem to happen after you eat a particular food. Anyway, erm, take this pamphlet, and it'll explain more about migraines.
MC Thanks.
Dr In the meantime, here's a prescription for tablets which

TAPESCRIPTS

you can take as soon as you feel a headache coming on. But please read the instructions carefully and don't take more than the recommended dose.
MC Fine.
Dr And come back in three to four weeks and we'll see how you've been getting on.
MC Thanks a lot.

Dialogue B
Dr Hello, Mrs Watson. What's wrong with John then?
MW Well, he's got this really sore throat and says it hurts when he swallows.
Dr Mhm. How long has he been like this?
MW A few days now.
Dr All right then, let's have a look. Now, John, just open your mouth wide and say 'Ah', and I'll have a look with my torch.
J Aaah.
Dr Mhmm, well, the back of your throat certainly looks red. Let me feel your neck. Mhmm, yes, there's some swelling there. I just need to look in your ears. Mhmm, mhmm, right, yes, they're a little red too. Well, Mrs Watson it looks like tonsillitis to me.
MW Oh dear.
Dr He needs a course of antibiotics.
MW Oh dear, this is the third time this year it's happened. Will he need to have his tonsils out?
Dr Erm, possibly, but we'll see how he gets on. If it happens again, we'll make an appointment with the hospital to see about having them removed.
MW Well, thank you Doctor. Come on, John.
Dr I hope you're better soon.
J Thank you.

Unit 18
Exercise 2: Whodunnit?
There were five people who could have killed Celia Mallinson. First, there was her husband, Donald Mallinson. He was obviously bored with her and he probably knew that she was having an affair with Dean. Then there was the daughter, Tessa, who hated her mother. Which brings us to the barman. He and Tessa were flirting, and this made Celia Mallinson angry. That's why she went outside - to look for them. I heard her threatening to get the young man fired if she found him with her daughter. Perhaps Celia Mallinson found Tessa and the barman together when she went outside? Now we come to Lawrence Dean, her former lover. She'd rejected him, and he'd booked into the hotel. He was angry and jealous, and he obviously wanted to cause trouble between Celia Mallinson and her husband Donald. And last of all there was the friend, Laura Pagett, a quiet sensible woman, not the type you would have thought to commit murder. But she too could have had a motive. She was planning to divorce her husband and take her share of the money out of her husband's business. Celia Mallinson had threatened to make trouble for Laura by telling Mr Pagett what she intended to do. None of them had alibis to cover the time of the murder: between roughly eleven o'clock when she left the hotel and quarter to twelve when her body was discovered. The only person who seemed in the clear was Mr Pagett. He had no motive for murdering Celia Mallinson and he didn't arrive at the hotel until after the police got here. He was driving down from London.

Exercise 3: The solution
The only person who seemed in the clear was Mr Pagett. He had no motive for murdering Celia Mallinson and he didn't arrive at the hotel until after the police got here. He was driving down from London. But if that was the case, why did the manager have trouble starting Pagett's car? The engine should have been warm if he'd just finished a long journey. According to Pagett, the car had only been standing 10 minutes. We know now, of course, what really happened. Mr Pagett arrived from London much earlier. He saw Celia Mallinson walking across the bridge. She was wearing a fur coat like his wife's and a fur hat which made it look as if she had dark hair. I thought the same when I first saw her. Pagett thought Celia was his wife, Laura. He knew she was planning to divorce him and he suspected she'd take her money with her. But if she died, he'd inherit her share of the business. So he parked the car, followed her, and hit her over the back of the head with a heavy torch. But it wasn't his wife; it was Celia Mallinson. He panicked and threw her body over the bridge. Then he waited until the body was found and the police had arrived. But meanwhile, of course, the engine of the car had cooled down. And if I hadn't seen the manager trying to start Pagett's car, he might have got away with it.

Unit 19
Exercise 2: Travellers' tales
Speaker 1
Oh, I love it. For one thing, the location is beautiful. It's on the sea, and the Bosphorus runs right through it, so on either side of the river you get wonderful views of the city across the water. The city has a wonderful atmosphere, and tremendous variety. I think often tourists are surprised because they expect it to be more traditional than it is. Of course, there are ancient buildings, like the Blue Mosque, but there is also a lot of construction going on - new buildings, new bridges, water mains, electricity cables, and so on. What I don't like about the city? Well, the pollution, I suppose. It's a big problem. And there are constant year-round water shortages. Commuting is difficult and so everyone wants to live in the city. That puts lots of pressure on the public transport system. They've built two bridges over the Bosphorus and that's helped a little, but there are still traffic jams in the centre of town. Visitors sometimes complain about the weather, but I don't mind it. It's hot and humid in the summer, but in the winter you even get some snow. It's varied, I suppose, like everything else in the city.

Speaker 2
Well, obviously the first thing that strikes you about it is that it's surrounded by water - it's incredibly beautiful. I like the size of the city - it's not too big and not too small. And the people are

TAPESCRIPTS

friendly, very friendly, particularly towards foreigners. The architecture is also very beautiful. I suppose anyone visiting the city has to see the really famous places like the Doge's Palace and St Mark's Square. Of course the city does have some problems. For example, it's very polluted and as a result the canals are smelly. I don't know - it's a strange city in some ways - very beautiful but sad at the same time. Because it's a very old city and it's in a state of decay - you feel in one sense that it's a city that's dying, beginning to lose a life of its own. It's rather like a museum really - full of old buildings and old people. I found it all rather sad.

Speaker 3

I like the people, they're absolutely fantastic. They're really alive, really friendly, really outgoing. It's probably the most exciting city I've ever been to - it's very chaotic, very colourful. The part that I really enjoyed was visiting the islands off the coast - it gives you a break from the city. But in the city itself it's well worth visiting the area around the polo ground and then obviously there's the statue of Christ on top of the mountain. And of course the Copacabana Beach is a big attraction. What I don't like about it is the fact that it really is a very, very poor city - you do see people who are really suffering and living in terrible conditions. It's also a very dangerous city - there's a lot of crime, because the people are so desperate. Of course, the two are related.

Speaker 4

I like the climate - hot summers and cold winters. And things are cheap - I like that too. It's a great place to shop. And the eating is good too. There are a lot of restaurants and the food is quite cheap. The best place to go to get a view of the city is er, Victoria Peak. And of course Aberdeen Harbour is very well-known. It's a nice place to visit, but I don't like working there - the pace is really fast. People don't relax, they work all year round. The main problem at the moment is worry about 1997. Crime is also a very serious problem. The housing situation is Ok - people tend to live on the outer islands now and the main island is used for offices and shopping.

Unit 20

Exercise 2: Born or made?

Part 1

I I was wondering about leadership qualities. What sort of qualities do you think a leader has to have?
P Well, first of all, there has to be a certain amount of intelligence. And whoever the leader is, charisma. That is, there has to be something interesting about them, something that makes other people notice them and respond to them. And then, they also need to act as if they believe that they are the leader.
I What do you mean?
P Well, I know some people in positions of leadership who appear to be very strong and creative, but inwardly they are very anxious and unsure of themselves. Outwardly they look as though they are in charge and comfortable.

I So you're saying that it's more important to look confident than it is to actually feel confident.
P Yes, though of course it's ideal to both look and feel confident.

Part 2

I I see. Do you think leadership ability may be developed, or is it something that we're born with?
P Well, both, really. First of all, the intelligence that you're born with is important. But after that, the family is very important. If your family want you to become a leader, then they will train you to become a leader, and you will be educated in that way - I was thinking about the Kennedy family.
I Mhmm, mhmm.
P But apart from intelligence, I don't think that the ability to lead is something that you're born with.
I Is there any way that we can develop our own leadership skills then?
P Yes. By watching someone that you admire and then behaving as they behave. That person might be a teacher, or a family member. It doesn't matter. Watch them and think, now why did they do that?

Part 3

I What can you tell me about different styles of leadership?
P First there's what we call a democratic leadership style. A democratic leader likes to include all the group members in the decision making, and they will change or adapt their own ideas to meet the needs of the group.
I Mhmm.
P The advantage of this type of leadership style, is that it gives power to the group members. The disadvantage is that sometimes the group members may not be sure who is in charge.
I Mhmm, mhmm, I see.
P And then the opposite leadership style is what I call authoritarian.
I Mhmm.
P The authoritarian type of leader is firm, definite, unbending - they don't want to give over power to the other members of the group. The advantage of this type of leadership style is that everyone knows who is in charge. The disadvantage is that the leader can be too set on their own ideas. They may not want to take advice and they can become cut off from what is actually happening in the group - the sort of 'I'm right and everyone else is wrong' type of attitude.
I So what sort of leadership style do you think is the best?
P Well, personally, I think the best leaders are not the ones that are stuck in any one leadership style. I think that the best leaders are able to combine the different leadership styles and use them where it's appropriate to use them.
I I see. Well, thank you very much.

Collins ELT
HarperCollins Publishers
77 - 85 Fulham Palace Road
London W6 8JB

© HarperCollins Publishers Ltd, 1991

All rights reserved. No part of this book may be reproduced, stored in a retrieval system or transmitted in any form or by any means, electronic, mechanical, photocopying, recording or otherwise, without the prior permission in writing of the publisher.

Acknowledgements

The publishers are grateful to the following for permission to reproduce the copyright material on the pages in the Student's Book indicated.

Ademma text (p 3) and ActionAid text (p 66) reproduced by kind permission of **ActionAid**; material from *The Book of Chinese Beliefs* by Frena Bloomfield (p 51) reproduced by permission of Arrow Books, Randon Century Group; first line of *Buckskin Run* by Louis L'Amour (p 35) reproduced by permission of Bantam Books; Bali text (p 21) adapted from *Face Values* with the permission of BBC Enterprises Ltd.; 'Zeebrugge girl who saved other lives' (p 9), Braille text (p 43), 'My brother put out the flames' (p 45) and Jane Stanbury text (p 46), all reproduced by kind permission of **Best** magazine; 'Consumer rights' (pp 18 and 70) reproduced from *Which?* and *Which? Way to Complain* by permission of the Consumer's Association; first line of *The Spy Who Came in from the Cold* by John le Carré (p 35), published by Hodder & Stoughton, reproduced by permission of David Higham Associates Ltd.; material from *Color Magic (Colour Your World)* by Frank Don (p 15) reprinted with permission of Destiny Books, a division of Inner Traditions International; 'Bid to save whales' (p 7) © The Guardian, reproduced by permission of Guardian News Service Ltd.; A good night's sleep (p 72) adapted from *Man, Myth and Magic*, Volume 2, Dreams, reproduced by kind permission of The Macdonald Group; 'The Mary Celeste' (p 58), from *The Encyclopaedia of the Strange*, © 1985 by Daniel Cohen. Reproduced by permission Marboro Books Corp.; information for 'The Greenhouse Effect' (p 32) reproduced by permission of **The Observer**; 'Youth Awards' (pp 10 and 68) reproduced by kind permission of the **National Council of YMCAs**; first line of *The Tree of Hands* by Ruth Rendell (p 35), © Kingsmarkham Enterprises Ltd. 1984. Reprinted by permission of the Peters, Fraser & Dunlop Group Ltd.; Palmyra text (p 37) from *Syria - Land of Contrasts* by Peter Lewis, Quartet Books Limited; 'Body language' text (p 1) from *Body Language* by Allan Pease, reproduced by permission of Sheldon Press; Brainsex quiz (p 19) adapted from the **Daily Mail**, and Murphy's Law (p 53) adapted from **You** magazine, both reproduced by permission of Solo Syndication and Literary Agency Ltd.; 'Holding on to tradition' (p 11), 'Back in space but doubts remain' (p 23) and Kennedy text (p 60) all reproduced by kind permission of **Spotlight** magazine; text (p 48) and 'Colour in your life' (p 69) from *Know Yourself Through Colour* by Marie Louise Lacy, and 'Dream talk' (p 28), and texts (p 54) from *Your Dreams and What They Mean* by Nerys Dee, all reproduced by permission of Thorsons; *A Cold and Frosty Morning* by June Thomson (p 35) reproduced by permission of June Thomson and Tessa Sayle Agency; 'Human chain drags whales from death in sea of blood' (p 7), Ian Brice text (p 33), body language text (p 41), snake text and Michael Webb text (p 44), 'Space ace, 14, set for lift-off' (p 52) and Reagan text (p 60) all reproduced by kind permission of **Today** newspaper; cartoon (p 8) reproduced by permission of United Feature Syndicate, Inc.

The publishers and author would like to express their particular admiration for Amanda Turner who died shortly after the Best of British Youth Awards ceremony, and their sympathy for her family.

First published 1991

ISBN 0 00 370506 4

Printed and bound in Great Britain by HarperCollinsManufacturing Glasgow
This Student's Book is accompanied by a Teacher's Book ISBN 0 00 370507 2 and a cassette ISBN 0 00 370508 0

Photographs

A shot in the dark (p 17); Ace Photo Agency (p 17); ActionAid/Liba Taylor (p 2); J Allan Cash Ltd (p 40); Art Directors Photo Library (pp 5, 15, 24, 40 x2); Associated Press (p 7); David Beatty/Susan Griggs Agency (p 15); Bernd Ducke-Eric Bach/Images Colour Library (p 15); Nigel Blythe/Cephas Picture Library (p 2); Camera Press London (p 39 x4); Camera Press/G Gwynfryn-Evans (p 17); Camera Press/Guy Flesch (p 2); Camera Press/David Steen (p 25); Colorific!/Jerry Irwin/Black Star (p 11); Mark Edwards/Still Pictures (p 31); Fred Espenak/Science Photo Library (p 23); Greg Evans Photo Library (pp 17, 40); Mary Evans Photo Library (p 38); Fukuhara Inc./West Light (p 21); Goldwater: Network (p 24); Grafenhain-Bach/Images Colour Library (p 21); Susan Griggs Agency/Dam Woolfitt (p 40); Hamleys, London (p 19); Robert Harding Associates/Walter Rawlings (p 25); Harvard College Observatory/Science Photo Library (p 23); Oliver Hatch (pp 3, 35); Hong Kong Tourist Board (p 22 x3); Hulton Deutsch Collection (p 38 x3); The Image Bank/JP Pienchot (p 2); Images Colour Library (pp 17, 33); Camilla Jessel (p 27); Frank Lane Picture Agency (p 5); Lifefile/Emma Lee (p 13); Lifefile/M Maidment (p 13); Lifefile/Ged Moxon (p 13 x2); Lifefile/Ray Ward (p 9); Lifefile/Jon Woodhouse (p 9); Norman Lomax Impact Photos (p 15); Hank Morgan/Science Photo Library (p 24); Photo Co-op (p 31); Photo Library International (p 24); Pictor International (pp 5, 17 x2); Pictures Colour Library (p 15 x2); Santiago Castrillon Photo Co-op (p 1); Spectrum Colour Library/V Sharp (p 31); Frank Spooner Pictures (pp 1, 23, 24); Tony Stone Worldwide (pp 5, 33); Tony Stone Worldwide/Julie Marcotte (p 21); Tony Stone Worldwide/John Starr (p 21); Tony Stone Worldwide/Billy Stickland (p 25); The Telegraph Colour Library (pp 5, 15 x2, 27, 31, 33); Viewfinder (p 9 x2); Visionbank (p 31); YMCA (p 10).

Illustrations

Phil Bannister; John Crawford Fraser; Peter Harper; Kevin Hauff; Robin Heighway-Bury; Andy Hill; Biz Hull; Jonno; Stan Kaminski; Stephen Player; Lynne Robertson; Chris Wadden; Nadine Wickenden; Emma Wilkinson.

The publishers have made every effort to contact owners of copyright. They apologise for any omissions, and if details are sent, will be glad to rectify these when the title is reprinted.

Design: Gregor Arthur

The author wishes to express her gratitude to the editors:
Judith Cunningham, Clare Leeds, Gabby Pritchard
and also to the following for their help:
Beth Hayward, Mike Lambert, Helen Cunningham, Cicero School of Languages and especially to Valerie Cunningham for her contribution to Unit 20.
Special thanks are due to Martyn Ellis and Jan Boldt, for their valuable comments.